God's Story Is My Story

ESSAYS
ON HEARING
AND TELLING
THE WORD

edited by Walter Wangerin Jr.

Evangelical Lutheran Church in America • Chicago

Library of Congress Cataloging-in-Publication Data

God's story is my story: essays on hearing and telling the word/
    edited by Walter Wangerin, Jr.
        p.   cm.
    Includes bibliographical references.
    ISBN 0-8066-3621-1 (alk. paper)
    1. Lutheran preaching.   I. Wangerin, Walter.
BX8074.P73G63 1997
251'.41—dc21   97-21581
                                                              CIP

The paper used in this publication meets the minimum requirements of American National Standard for Information Sciences—Permanence of Paper for Printed Library Materials, ANSI Z329.48-1984.

Manufactured in the U.S.A.

01   00   99   98   97   1   2   3   4   5   6   7   8   9   10

Contents

Preface   v
by Walter Wangerin Jr.

Foreword   vii
by H. George Anderson, presiding bishop of the
Evangelical Lutheran Church in America

HEARING

Listening for the Breath of Prayer   1
by Terry L. Bowes

TELLING

It Is Jesus   8
by Herbert W. Chilstrom

Over Mere Words the Holy Spirit Hovers   17
by John Vannorsdall

HEARING

This Story Is Mine   23
by Karris Golden

TELLING

I Long to Speak Jesus   30
by Susan Briehl

Come Over and Help Us   38
by Conrad M. Thompson

HEARING

This Is Most Certainly True!   45
by William E. Diehl

TELLING

Hearing One Another into Speech   53
    by Barbara Lundblad

I Love to Tell the Story   62
    by Richard A. Jensen

God Speaks to Doubters, Too   72
    by Barbara Berry-Bailey

HEARING

Gathered to Hear the Living Voice   81
    by Gail McGrew Eifrig

TELLING

Speaking Is Our Holy Task   88
    by April Ulring Larson

God's Love Story Is Dialogue   94
    by Walter Wangerin Jr.

Preface

L uther called it the living voice of the gospel. Whenever people proclaim the mighty acts of God's salvation, whenever people hear the good news of God's love—whenever these things happen, we lay claim to Jesus Christ, and we are changed. In telling the story and in hearing it, the story becomes ours. God's story is our story.

This book is about the relationships that are forged as the Word is proclaimed. What do preachers feel about preaching? What are the dimensions of the tender relationship between the preacher and the listener—between the Word and the hearer of the Word? Some who have written for these pages are telling us why they listen, how vital is this Word for life, how life is changed when the Word is proclaimed with power, how they recognize themselves in the story and say, "Amen!" Others tell us why they preach and what they trust happens to people as they preach. This book is about the holiness of proclaiming the gospel.

I have been the host of *Lutheran Vespers* for a little more than two years now, the fifth preacher and host in the past fifty years. We receive several hundred letters every week from listeners, and know them to be members of many denominations (or of no church at all), every age group, every marital status. The audience is broad. It is the preaching and the listening that makes a spiritual bond among us. And so the idea of this book. Indirectly, it will honor the role that *Lutheran Vespers* has played for half a century, preaching, existing by the preaching and the listening only. But most importantly, this book proposes a meeting of the minds and souls of the preacher and the listener during this elemental event when God's Word is the bond between them.

Walter Wangerin Jr.

Foreword

J'm very proud of the way that *Lutheran Vespers* enables our church to reach beyond the walls of our congregations and go into the homes and automobiles of people who otherwise might not have the opportunity to hear God's word and the Lutheran understanding of the faith. Whether listeners are at home or not, God's word can reach them through radio.

Lutheran Vespers also reaches many of our members who aren't able to be in church. I know that Walt Wangerin thinks about these people as he prepares his messages. When he was interviewing me once, he said, "Suppose you were an eighty-year-old in a nursing home. What hope is there in this passage for you?" He specifically imagines the circumstances of out-of-the-ordinary persons who are lonely or not directly connected to the church. Radio ministry can do that.

In addition to the unchurched, the "accidental" listeners in cars—perhaps we can call them occasional visitors—and the homebound, there are many people who listen to *Lutheran Vespers* as they get ready to go to church. Even though they will attend a service, it gives them a theological and musical start on the worship of the day. Or, depending upon the timing of the programming, it's their midweek service.

Any sermon, anywhere, is an opportunity for the church to take the time-honored, tested traditions and stories that we know so well and reclothe them in circumstances and experiences that are close to the lives of hearers. For example, much of the biblical material comes out of a nomadic and pastoral society. Many of our people do not live in such surroundings today. So a sermon helps people understand that when the Bible talks about a seed falling in the ground, or about sheep and shepherds, it is really showing us that Scripture has

something to do with homeless people, or with children who
are not active in church. This is why Walt's sermons start in
the lives of people rather than in the first century. It is possible
through a sermon to help someone see that they are not the
first person who has walked where they are. Rather, there is a
whole history of God's people who have had similar experiences in different ages and different circumstances. Suddenly
the hearer says, "I have company on this road. There is a path
here. It's not a total wilderness."

Then there is the *Lutheran Vespers* blend of music that uses
contemporary musical settings but with familiar texts. Again,
music is a way to link tradition with the here and now. Like
hearing the gospel for the first time, the music is heard in a
fresh way, too.

Above all, it is remarkable how a mass medium such as radio
can be so personal. I remember a radio preacher telling me that
when he prepared his radio message, he would "always think of
somebody standing there at an ironing board. I just talk to that
person rather than to the whole audience." *Lutheran Vespers*
speaks that language.

H. George Anderson
Presiding Bishop
Evangelical Lutheran Church in America

Listening for the Breath of Prayer

by Terry L. Bowes

*I*mmovable and implacable as a boulder, the nurse stolidly blocked my entrance into the intensive-care cubicle. She stopped me more with her voice than her body, though I found that both impeded my stumbling, head-long progress. Over her voice I could hear the steady beeps of monitors and the thumps of a respirator. Over her shoulder, I could barely make out a figure lying still in the bed, lit by the dim glow of a fluorescent lamp. It was four o'clock in the morning.

Six hours earlier, a pair of sheriff's deputies, a representative of the coroner's office, and a victim's assistance volunteer had appeared at my door to notify me that my twenty-year-old daughter, Melissa, had been killed in an automobile accident. Ann, her best friend and passenger, had been airlifted to the region's finest trauma hospital in Denver. Ann had suffered massive head injuries. Her condition was critical.

The ironic fact was that Melissa and Ann had been on their way to our house to try to lift my spirits when the accident

1

occurred. Three years earlier, to the week, our older daughter had taken her own life, and I was immersed in the suffocating sorrow and might-have-beens that accompany such anniversaries. Instead of opening the door to the bright eyes and irresistible energy of two lively college students, I opened the door to messengers of death who told me to prepare for yet another walk up the hill to bury yet another daughter. As they talked to me in low, strained voices, I pulled the dark, dank cloak of grief more tightly around myself and knew that I couldn't survive this time. Like Rachel weeping for her children, I simply could not be consoled.

As the predawn house filled with brave friends, I was only dimly aware of phone calls to and from the hospital. Perhaps, just perhaps, the identities of the two girls in the mangled car had been confused. Perhaps, just perhaps, Melissa lived. I should come and see.

The nurse's voice was calm and even. She was determined not to let me enter the room until I had all the facts. The girl in the bed had massive head and facial injuries. She was on a ventilator. I shouldn't be shocked by what I saw. I murmured promises not to make a scene, but the nurse clearly did not believe me and continued. The girl was unconscious, she explained, largely due to the sedatives she was receiving. She had suffered closed head injuries, but the extent of brain damage could not be determined yet. Miraculously, she had no other injuries—no broken bones other than in her skull and face, no internal injuries. She would live. She might or might not be Melissa.

Finally, after peering into my face to assess how much, if anything, I comprehended, the nurse turned and led me into the room. I had prepared myself to find Ann, but this swollen purple face didn't look a thing like Ann. Perhaps it was wishful thinking, but the still, young woman resembled Melissa.

"Her hands," I said. "Let me see her hands." I lost patience as the nurse fumbled to unwrap the restraining mittens from the patient's hands. I moved to the foot of the bed, lifted the sheet, and looked at those precious feet, calloused from hours of playing basketball. I gripped a foot in each hand and remembered my vow to remain calm. "It's Melissa," I whispered. I could hear the intake of breath of the friends and intensive-care staff who had accompanied me into the room. "It's Melissa," the word went out.

➤ ➤ ➤

From the tiny window in Melissa's room I watched the sun rise on that fifth day in Lent. I watched the dawn illumine a statue of Jesus that presided over a garden bed of ready-to-burst daffodils. One overzealous daffodil had bloomed before the rest; its vibrant blossom brushed gently against the hem of Jesus' stone robe. At that moment it was not one but every Easter sermon that I had ever heard that flooded my soul. Suddenly it was all so real, so palpable, resounding with truth—the faithful women setting out before dawn to perform their grim task of love; the stone rolled away; the empty tomb; the fright, grief, confusion, guilt, disbelief. As the purple sky streaked with pink that morning, I thought of Mary Magdalene clutching Jesus' feet when she recognized his voice, and, with her, I wept with joy. At that Easter moment, for Mary Magdalene and for me, the stories of the master teacher connected with my life experience and suddenly they made transformational, transforming sense. We would never be the same.

No one sermon can prepare us for the surprising gift and challenge of life, and no one sermon can make the bone-grinding work of grief more palatable. However, together, in combination, sermons add up to more than their sum. Blessed are the faithful hearers of the Word for they have received the code to help them translate life. They have received resources to endure, take courage, find joy. In the hearing we are trained to find the sacred in the ordinary; we are prompted to accept and respond to God's gifts with joy and thanksgiving.

Melissa's story is the stuff that daytime talk television is made of. Increasingly, accounts of the power of prayer and miraculous near-death experiences appear in mainstream print and TV newsmagazines in a wave of tantalizing spirituality. Yet neither Melissa nor I feel any kinship to the people who share their dramatic stories and come to the conclusion that God chose for them to live "for a reason." Oh, yes, we certainly feel that we have experienced a miracle and know that we have been touched by the power of prayer. Melissa recovered completely, finished college, married, earned a master's degree. Miraculous, indeed, yet at the same time we remember that lovely Ann died and that her parents and brother grieve.

How can any of us put together all those disparate elements of prayer and miracle, loss and grief, and the meaning of life and death in a way that, if it cannot make sense, is at least bearable? How does one resist sliding into the easy temptation to be fatalistic and smug? I find the strength to wrestle with the tough questions every day because good preachers along the way have taught me to notice one yellow daffodil brushing against the hem of Jesus' robe.

One of the unexpected blessings of serving as a lay leader in all three expressions of the church—congregation, synod, and churchwide—is the opportunity that I've had to hear preaching in a wide variety of settings and from a wide range of voices. Which preachers—what preaching—of the Word stand out in my memory and in my living, and why? Who are the faces and the voices who have held the gospel out to me in ways that continue to encourage and challenge me to step out in faith? What is it that beckons me to take the terrifying leap from the predictable, controlled, and comfortable to the unknown, uncontrolled, uncomfortable place where I can grow in faith and surrender to God's will?

I've learned to listen for that breath of prayer that sighs through the words of the faithful preacher. Good preaching is incarnational. Give me the words, the images that capture my

mind, lodge in my heart, and nurture my soul. Give me words
and images that connect to my life so that the word of God
reveals the Word of God for me.

I easily can bring those great images to mind. It was star-
tlingly uplifting for me, as a grieving mother, to hear Ron
Swenson of Augustana Lutheran Church in Denver, Colorado,
describe All Saints' Day as a "grand family reunion."

Every Christmas Eve I recall James Cobb of First Lutheran
Church in Norfolk, Virginia, recounting the story of observing
the child of a family in his parish as the child gazed intently at
the Nativity scene on the family's table. After a long period of
contemplation, the preschooler turned to his mother and
demanded, "Why aren't they moving?"

Melanie McRae of St. Luke Lutheran Church in
Bloomington, Minnesota, gave me another image of childlike
theology in a sermon in which she recounted watching her
four-year-old daughter, Ana, help her father plant a garden. Ana
looked skeptically at the small seeds that she and Scott were
carefully laying in rows and covering with dirt. As they worked
together, her father, also a pastor, was describing the resurrection of Jesus to her. Finally Ana sat back on her heels, looked at
her tall and lean father, tenderly brushed a strand of hair from
his forehead, and said, "I believe that, Daddy. But I don't believe
that this ever will be a cucumber."

The word "joy" always reminds me of Barbara Lundblad of
Our Saviour Atonement Lutheran Church in New York City.
She described a surprise encounter with joy on a busy New
York corner as she watched a blind woman tap her stick all
around herself in a circle. Then, laying the stick down, the
woman raised her hands above her head and did a jig in the
midst of the crowd, grinning the entire time.

Every Easter from now on, I will recall Walt Wangerin's 1996
Easter sermon on the radio program *Lutheran Vespers,* when he
described Easter as a "bright island in life, when, for a moment,
sadness can stall and stop. It doesn't mean that what nagged me

yesterday or what is going to be required of me tomorrow is gone. But it does mean that the teeth in these things, the teeth of certain kinds of responsibilities cannot chew or bite me today, and therefore cannot chew or bite me forever."

Powerful preaching gives me the power to resist the glittering and the glib that passes itself off as spirituality today. Feel-good spirituality assures me that I will not be held accountable, offers easy explanations about pain and loss, and holds out promises of success and inner peace. The vast smorgasbord of modern spirituality offers the alluring option of passing up *hoc est corpus meum* ("This is my body") in favor of hocus pocus. Powerful preaching, on the other hand, points me irrevocably to Christ and a theology of the cross and an empty tomb.

Powerful preaching opens my eyes to the needs of my neighbor. It expands my answer to the question, "Who is my neighbor?" It points to the evils and sins in this world and in my heart, evils such as racism, sexism, ageism, and classism. Powerful preaching calls me to repentance, risk, and action. Challenging sermons are not at all comfortable. I dread hearing them. But oh, how I need them!

I have found that some sermons seem to replay themselves in my mind just when I need them, often years after I have heard them. While I might not recognize powerful preaching at the time, I do instinctively sniff out poor preaching. I've experienced some charming shenanigans from the pulpit. There is a difference between a good sermon and a nifty little speech. There is a difference between proclaiming the gospel and delivering pop psychology that concludes with a bowed head and pious "Amen." I have heard brilliant sermons delivered by people who should be authors. I would buy every one of their books as soon as they hit the bookstores. Yet their sermons ring hollow. It's not a matter of style or delivery; it is a matter of failing to provide me with a glimpse of God.

Satisfying as it is, it is not enough that I lay out my expectations of preachers. I bear responsibility to be an active partici-

pant in the preaching-hearing process. I must be present—
physically, mentally, and spiritually. I must be willing to grow in
maturity and discernment.

I had an enlightening and frightening experience recently. As
I drove my rental car from one city in Florida to another, I fumbled to find a radio station to accompany me on my drive. As
the needle moved up the AM and FM bands, I encountered
three different independent Christian radio stations. The topic
on all three stations, discussed by different people in different
ways, was the same one: a scathing attack on women in national
government. I realized then that, while the three stations said
that they were independent, they shared an agenda and had
received information from a single source. In the midst of that
choppy turbulence on the radio airwaves, *Lutheran Vespers*
appears as a fluorescent life vest. Do we truly appreciate the gift
that we have been given and hold out to the world?

So keep preaching, Walt and faithful pastors everywhere.
Pray your sermons, and I'll be there to hear you and call out,
"Amen." You may never know how the seeds you plant take
root, but do know that your proclamation makes a difference.
You connect the gospel story to personal story, and in that
transforming act, we will never be the same.

➤ ➤ ➤

*Terry L. Bowes serves as interim executive director of Women of the
Evangelical Lutheran Church in America and is a former member of the
Church Council of the Evangelical Lutheran Church in America.*

TELLING

It Is Jesus

by Herbert W. Chilstrom

Someone asked Bob Hope at his ninetieth birthday party what makes a great comedian. Without a moment's hesitation he replied, "It's simple—the material and the delivery—as simple as that."

I'm a long way from my ninetieth year—in fact, only a year into retirement as I write this. But even from this early stage of the years of retrospection, I would say much the same about preaching—that it's "the material and the delivery." For Bob Hope the material is, of course, a good story. He's always looking for that story or punch line that he can use in his routine.

The material is the gospel

For the preacher the material is first and foremost the gospel. It is the good news. It is Jesus. Not *about* Jesus. It *is* Jesus. It is the simple story that "God so loved the world. . . ."

The mark of a great preacher is that he or she knows that the source for that good news is in the written Word of God, the Bible. I come out of a tradition that always accented the impor-

8

tance of preaching that is solidly anchored in the Holy Scriptures. I was taught that the purpose of a sermon is twofold—to help our listeners know what the Bible says and to help them know how it applies to their world. As Krister Stendahl put it, preaching is to tell folks *what is said* and *what it says.* It's the same idea that Reinhold Niebuhr had in mind when he remarked that we ought to preach with the Bible in one hand and the newspaper in the other.

Now that I am more often on the listening side of the sermon, it's my impression that preachers of the Word often pass too quickly from the Bible to the newspaper. That is, we give short shrift to careful reflection on the scripture readings for a given Sunday and make the sermon into a series of stories or applications that relate in some loose way to a topic that may or may not have some connection with the scripture readings for the day.

What good preaching boils down to is that the preacher begins by looking deeply and carefully at the assigned texts for the day or the occasion. There is good reason why the pericope cycle of Sunday readings has survived over the years. It gives us the balance we need for preaching. And it gives our hearers a full acquaintance with every part of the Bible. I'm convinced that those who come to church want to know, more than anything else, what the Bible has to say to them. That means that the preacher must spend his first and most important sermon preparation time in wrestling with the texts for the day, asking the questions, "What are these texts about? Why were they preserved in the canon of Scripture? What was God trying to say to them when these words were spoken and written?" As the answers to these questions begin to emerge from one's study of the Bible, one then can begin to ask, "What is God saying to me? What does God want me to say to those who will hear me? Is there a prophetic word I need to speak, a need in our community and world that must be confronted?"

During my twenty years as a bishop I preached in thousands of different settings. The compliment I savored most was when

a pastor said after the service that he or she was surprised that I
had preached on the text for that Sunday instead of pushing for
some special cause of the synod or the Evangelical Lutheran
Church in America. A cause never saved a soul or turned a life
around. The gospel does!

Simply eloquent

As for the second element in Bob Hope's formula—delivery—
the advice of William Penn still stands: "Speak properly and in
as few words as you can, but always plainly; for the end of
speech is not ostentation but to be understood." Simplicity and
ostentation are opposites; simplicity and eloquence are not.

There are those who think that the "Mission90" video series
What Does It Mean to Be a Christian? was one of the more sig-
nificant things I did during my time as presiding bishop of the
Evangelical Lutheran Church in America. If that is true, the
secret may be in the simplicity of the series. My goal was to
develop a "visual catechism," a series of presentations that
would set out in the most basic ways the fundamental aspects
of our Lutheran understanding of the Christian faith. I remember wondering to myself if I had leaned too far in the direction
of simplicity. "Will these tapes be used once and then relegated
to the storage shelf," I asked myself. In the years that followed it
became apparent that the strength of the series was, in fact, its
simplicity. As I encountered folks here and there who testified
to the help they had received in understanding what it meant to
be a Christian, I was reminded again that we do our best work
as preachers and teachers when we take the essential truths of
the gospel and present them in clear, understandable ways to
our hearers.

That certain energy

When Bob Hope spoke of delivery, he hardly meant that all that
is needed is to stand in front of an audience and tell a story. He
brings with him a certain charisma or energy that makes all the

difference. Someone else could tell the same stories and they would fall flat. But when Hope tells them it's apparent that no one enjoys them as much as he. He and his stories are one. This is a quality common to all effective writers and performers. When Annie Dillard advised other budding writers on the most essential elements of her discipline, she said, "Write as if you were dying. At the same time, assume you write for an audience consisting solely of terminal patients. That is, after all, the case. What would you begin writing if you knew you would die soon? What could you say to a dying person that would not enrage by its triviality?"[1]

In my judgment, this is the most important element in effective preaching. It begins with the conviction of Paul, "I have been crucified with Christ; and it is no longer I who live, but it is Christ who lives in me" (Galatians 2:19b-20a). I'm not sure I understood much about this when I first started my ministry as a young pastor. I had been through the seminary. I had all the academic qualifications. I had been approved by the elders of the church as fit for being ordained as a pastor. But I'm afraid the description that Halford E. Luccock, professor of preaching at Yale Divinity School, once made fit me all too well. "It is a great mistake in aeronautics," he observed, "to build transport planes to carry a load greater than the wing power. The average student leaves the seminary with more load than wing power to carry it."

Molded in the crucible of life

It was only in the crucible of life, as I wrestled with ambiguities, as I struggled with my inadequacies in every aspect of ordained ministry, as I battled with the uncertainties of cancer in myself and my wife, as I fell toward despair over the loss of a son, as I fought to preserve my integrity in speaking my convictions in the face of intense opposition, as I did battle with temptations to pride and lust and selfishness—it was only as I was driven repeatedly to the cross of Christ that I began to realize that I had nothing to bring with me to the pulpit but a word that God is with us, that God will not forsake us no matter how desperate the situation may be. Marcus Dods (1834–1909), noted author, once wrote of his discouragement at trying to be a minister of the gospel—words that most of us who are called to ordination easily can identify with:

> No day passes without strong temptation to give up, on the ground that I am not fitted for pastoral work; writing sermons is often the hardest labor, visiting is terrible. I often stand before a door unable to ring or knock—sometimes I have gone away without entering. A lowness of spirit that it costs me a great deal to throw off is the consequence of this, and a real doubt whether it would not be better for myself and all whom it may concern that I should at once look for some work that I could overtake.

In time the cloud lifted for Dods, as it does for us. On another occasion, having risen from his slough of despond, he wrote that "faith is the firm persuasion that these things are so. And he who at once knows the magnitude of these things . . . must be fined with a joy that makes him independent of the world, with an enthusiasm which must seem to the world like insanity." The brightness of that joy could only come to him because he had been to its dark side of despair.

My good friend and former bishop Harold Lohr would sometimes say of a younger pastor, "He'll be very good some day—after he suffers a little." I understood what he meant. No, he had no desire to see someone suffer in any way. Yet he knew that it is only in the long, dark nights of the soul, when we feel absolutely abandoned and when we have exhausted all of our own resources, that we learn to trust God's promises. And he knew that this quality—this energy—does not come to us merely through reading and study, important as they are. It comes only when the pastor has stood with the psalmist and has cried out, "My soul is full of troubles, and my life draws near to Sheol" (Psalm 88:3).

The style is you

Now that my wife, Corinne, and I are retired, we travel a good deal and find ourselves in different churches on many Sundays of the year. Within moments of the beginning of the service we can tell whether the pastor has this energy of which I speak. It has nothing to do with style. The pastor may be very soft-spoken or very forceful. She, like Aimee Simple McPherson, may have a robust voice that needs no amplification. He, like Phillips Brooks, may have a rather weak and raspy voice that one must strain to hear. Physical shape has nothing to do with this energy. I have sensed it in the most diminutive or the lack of it in the most physically overpowering. How can I describe it?

Maybe American novelist Katherine Anne Porter (1890–1980), in her comments on writing, has the answer:

> The style is *you*. Oh, you can cultivate a style I suppose, if you like. But . . . it remains a cultivated style. It remains artificial and imposed, and I don't think it deceives anyone. In the end, you do not create a style. You work, and develop yourself; your style is an emanation of your own being.

Do I make my point? Unless we go to the pulpit as those who have been crucified with Christ, as dying women and men preaching to dying listeners, as persons full of the energy of our convictions—unless we do this, the most highly polished and doctrinally correct sermon likely will fall on deaf ears.

The fundamentals of preaching

In my early ministry two books stood out among many as my guides to becoming a more effective preacher. First, there was Paul Scherer's *For We Have This Treasure* (New York: Harper & Brothers, 1944). In answer to the question "What is to be the content of our preaching?" Scherer said there are three things. First, we must give to our hearers "a greater God than any they have yet imagined for themselves." We know too much about life and the world and too little about God, said Scherer. And the first thing we should know about God is that God seeks us long before we begin to think about seeking God. God always takes the initiative and makes a decision for us. That needs to be said again and again in a religious culture that blares on and on about "finding God" and "making a decision" for Jesus Christ.

Second, said Scherer, we must preach boldly about "the tragic estate of the human soul." This is the question asked more than two decades ago by Karl Menninger, psychiatrist and author, but still relevant today: "Whatever became of sin?" Scherer reminded us that Jesus treated evil as fact, not fiction. Though we are made in the image of God and "a little lower than God (Psalm 8:5)," we are part of a fallen humanity that is in rebellion against God, both individually and as a human family. Once we admit to our brokenness we can begin to affirm our worth, says Scherer. We can call to the redeemed to stand tall and to allow God to mold them into what God wants them to be in the world.

The third thing that must be a part of all preaching, said Scherer, is to center every sermon in "the gospel of God concerning his Son" (Romans 1:1, 3). Scherer underscored the point I made earlier:

> The glad, good news is not *about* Jesus; it *is* Jesus—who judges life, ransoms life, and sets life upright on its feet again. It is not a concept; it is a power. It is not a formula or a dogma or a system, but a presence which still moves on in the dangerous vanguard of human life.... Let me beseech you therefore, wherever you take your text, make across country, as fast as ever you can, to him![2]

The other book that I treasured as a younger pastor was Andrew Blackwood's *The Growing Minister* (New York: Abingdon Press, 1960). What I have described as energy is defined by Blackwood as "Christian personality." He takes his lead from Phillips Brooks's definition of preaching as "bringing the truth through personality." Blackwood observed that leading public worship "tests the power of a [person's] personality." By this he meant that conducting a service and preaching a sermon are more than standing in front of a congregation. Unless one brings feeling—energy—into one's role as public leader, the worshipers and listeners likely will go home without having come to grips with the power of the gospel. All of one's God-given abilities must be put to work in the public leadership of worship. Everything—preparing the prayers, choosing the hymns, rehearsing the responsive reading, practicing the sermon—all of these call for an investment of emotion as well as intellect, said Blackwood. In other words, the investment of energy begins with the preparation for public worship and carries right through to the benediction. A good pastor should be completely exhausted by the end of the worship service.

Blackwood cited with approval the Treatise *Concerning the Religious Affections* by Jonathan Edwards. Although Edwards stands with the most intellectual preachers in American church history, he argued in this treatise that the heart has more to do with effective preaching than the head. Judging from the response to Edwards's preaching, it is clear that he invested his entire heart and soul in the task.[3]

Preaching for the new millennium

Is there any hope that we can restore the pulpit to the importance it claimed in earlier times? Is there a better way to accomplish the same thing? Must we do radical surgery on our worship patterns and preaching styles in order to hold the attention of a people who are entertained all hours of the day and night with a flick of the television switch? I have no easy answers. I only know that the human heart always will need to hear that Word that only the church has to give—a Word that points us to a God bigger than we imagined, that calls us to accountability for our sin, that points us to Christ as our only hope.

The pulpit is the prow

Although he is a fictional character, I hold the old Rev. Mapple in *Moby Dick* as my ideal. Herman Melville describes how Mapple mounts the pulpit in the seaside chapel. Having been "replenished by the meat and wine of the Word," this faithful man of God is ready to bring that Word to his hearers. The pulpit, writes Melville, is like the prow of a ship—as all pulpits should be.

> The pulpit is ever this earth's foremost part. All the rest comes in its rear. The pulpit leads the world. From thence it is the storm of God's quick wraths is first described and the bow must bear its earliest brunt. From these it is the God of breezes fair or foul is first invoked for favorable winds. Yes, the world's a ship on its passage out, and not a voyage complete. And the pulpit is its prow.

On one occasion Mapple is preaching about Jonah. What he says becomes the model for any sermon:

> Jonah did the Almighty's bidding. And what was that, shipmates? To preach the truth in the face of falsehood. That was it. And woe to that pilot of the living God who slights it. Woe to him whom this world charms from Gospel duty. Woe to him who seeks to please rather than to appall. Woe to him whose good name means more to him than goodness. Woe to him who would not be true even though to be false were salvation.

Indeed, Bob Hope had a point. It's really very simple—good material and good delivery. We have the material—the gospel. Do we have the delivery—the energy—to bring it to our hearers with power and love?

Herbert W. Chilstrom is the former presiding bishop of the Evangelical Lutheran Church in America, a former bishop of the Minnesota Synod of the Lutheran Church in America, and a teacher of New Testament.

Endnotes

1. Annie Dillard, *Three by Annie Dillard* (New York: HarperCollins Publishers, 1990), 590. Originally published as *The Writing Life* (Harper & Row, Publishers, 1989).
2. Paul Scherer, *For We Have This Treasure* (New York: Harper & Brothers, 1944).
3. Andrew Blackwood, *The Growing Minister* (New York: Abingdon Press, 1960).

Over Mere Words the Holy Spirit Hovers

by John Vannorsdall

I can furrow my brow if I wish. It doesn't make any difference. I can smile, shake my fist, tug at my ear, raise an eyebrow. It makes no difference. Beyond the double-glazed window the producer is eating a sandwich and the engineer is drifting. What I see is a microphone in my face and my manuscript on a table covered with soft green. No one sees me.

But they say that somewhere out there, in their cars, kitchens, and bathrooms, hundreds of thousands of people are listening, or partly listening, to the words I speak, the sound of my voice, the story that I have to tell. It's an impossible situation, of course. I can't actually speak with thousands of unseen and unknown people unless I limit myself to vacuous generalities. So I choose one person. I have something to share with this one person, and the others, if they be there, are welcome to overhear.

The listener
Who is this person with whom I, the radio preacher, have chosen to speak? He or she is always a cousin to the self. Together we see or imagine winter birches bent, are in awe and lonely under the

canopy of the night sky, are together asked our meaning by the
pounding surf, are quieted by moonlight on the water.

We are, this other and I, people who once ran for the sheer joy
of it, with the wind in our faces. We danced and marveled at the
warmth of another's embrace. We are those who were elected
once—at times not chosen—and the exhilaration of winning
and the down of losing are with us as we begin our conversation.

We are, the two of us, woven into a cultural fabric that cannot be ignored. Around us, sensed rather than seen, are the very
poor, always in debt and in trouble. Around us are the very rich,
both sensed and seen, those who have made reservations and
don't stand in lines, whose cars always start. We, the listener and
I, are neither poor nor rich, which leaves us unclear about who
we are, and social issues become confusing. It is hard to know
how to vote.

Neither I nor my listener killed Jews in central Europe. We
did not drop the bomb, riot in Belgrade, or slaughter Tutsis. We
did not own slaves. Nevertheless, cruelty slumbers within us.
We know that. Sometimes it comes awake with a yawn and we
tremble in self-recognition.

For all the certainty that the Lutheran radio preacher may
project, there is no great religious gulf between preacher and
listener. Both are aware of their mortality, and both wonder
whether there ever will be an end to human sorrow. Both long
to love and be loved, and both search for something holy and
self-transcending to give meaning to their lives. The listener
may have no relationship to the church, have never been baptized, and yet he or she shares with the preacher these percep-
tions and longings.

The preacher

What then occurs when these cousins share the intimacy of a
radio sermon? The preacher takes some aspect of the Christian
gospel and lays it in the midst of the life of the listener. It is as
simple, and as difficult, as that.

That the preacher centers his witness in the gospel is a matter of both personal commitment and professional responsibility. If the preacher does not believe that the gospel is the most substantive and compelling truth about human origins and destiny, human bondage and human freedom, then he or she should be excused from preaching. The matters to be shared are too important and this media too intimate to tolerate deception. The preacher also is bound to gospel preaching by his or her commitment to the church. This is what we were called to do in our ordination. If not ordained, then this is what we were called to do when we agreed to represent the church on the air.

The witness

One of the strengths and difficulties in all preaching is that we are given normative ways of saying the gospel. The witness is embedded in the Hebrew and Greek Scriptures. The liturgy of the church and its music, prayers, and celebrations are all rooted in the imagery of the Scriptures, and the imagery makes its universal claims through the particularities of the cultures that gave the writings their present shape.

To ignore or abandon the scriptural imagery is not an option. The story of creation, the giving of the law, the judgments and promises of the prophets, the birth of Christ, the parables from Christ's ministry, his death and resurrection— these events and teachings are the foundation of our present witness. These Scriptures must be read, rehearsed, and learned. Every preacher is committed to this task.

There are those who say that the public reading or telling of these Scriptures is effective in and of itself. And that's true to at least some degree. Preaching, however, is something else. It is to lay the ancient story within the images and meanings of the current hearer. The preacher's work is not to tell this listener what he or she should or must believe. The work of both preacher and hearer is to explore together the myths, stories,

and historical events concerning the creator God, and to share
what is whispered in the wind and proclaimed in thunder,
stone, and crosses. Our task is to understand Jesus Christ as the
Word of God in such a serious way that we take our own words
about God seriously, both rejoicing in and fearful of the power
of God's Word and the power of human speech.

The enemy of all preaching is the generalities that become
trap doors through which escapes the work of exploring the
meaning of a text and the hearer falls into numbed disinterest.
For example, the word "salvation" both says it all and says nothing. Rather, since both the preacher and the listener have been
lost, the preacher re-creates that experience. Together they
remember the time in a crowded department store when, small
and alone in waves of noise and strangers, they sought a loved
face and were found and embraced.

Don't tell me that God loves me. Remind me of the time
when I made a fool of myself at a public meeting and, after the
meeting had ended and the people had left, I stood there bleed-
ing and ashamed. Tell me about the Word in human form who
returned to put his arm upon my shoulder and invited me for
coffee.

Don't tell me that God forgives my sins for Christ's sake. I
know my angers, lusts, and many stupidities. I know how self-
interest warps my relationships every day of my life. But I am
working on it. On the other hand, if you gently lead me into my
complicity in racial stereotyping, in the consumption of oil, the
times when I vote my interests against the poor, then I know
that "working on it" never will suffice. My freedom from dis-
honesty and the restoration of my peace can be only a gift of
the God I so deeply offend.

So the preacher searches herself or himself, imagines the
experiences of the listener, and with well-chosen words creates
images that evoke recognition in the listener. The images are
never too detailed because the listener needs room to provide
those details that most closely fit his or her needs and percep-

tions. It is a delicate sharing that does not insist that the hearer have exactly the same experience as the preacher, but provides enough suggestion to serve as a bridge between the biblical text and the hearer's world of joy and loss.

Aptness

An image is most effective if it is apt, if it accurately and appropriately illumines the text, the witness to be shared. If the sermon's conversation is close to home—holding up small things, family matters, personal images—then to suddenly shift to a story that takes place on the streets of Calcutta will scramble the communication. The language of the sermon can be inept if it becomes so coarse that the listener is uncomfortable or so elevated and poetic that the preacher is distanced from the hearer.

Preaching is always an oral event. The preacher will recognize distracting words and phrases by saying a paragraph aloud, perhaps in the presence of a family member or a friend. For example, it may be that "an apple" is enough, allowing the listener to choose the color. "A dusty road" is a cliché and might better become "Main Street."

Fussiness in language and imagery is not helpful, but to ignore the aptness with which we say the gospel limits or mars the event.

Preparation

Preachers have different gifts, and imagination may be one that is limited or undeveloped. It certainly helps to read widely, everything from the local paper to Jon Hassler. It's not a matter of gathering quotations. It's a matter of adding to one's own experience the meanings of human life that others explore and share in their writings. It may be more important for preachers to take their continuing education in the field of literature than in theology or parish management. Storytelling, which depends upon the creation of images, is an art that is learned. It is practiced every time we tell another about something that has happened. The person who takes preaching seriously is one who is intentional in developing this capacity.

Consequence

Radio sermons are far from the wholeness that is the assembly of believers. There is no Lord's Supper or Baptism, voices are not raised together in hymns and prayers, and the face of the preacher cannot be seen. Nevertheless, the gospel is shared in words and images created by words, and is laid in the manger of the daily lives of tens of thousands of people. The consequences of such preaching are mostly unknown, but the biblical witness is to be trusted. Out of this so modest preaching God brings forth faith and understanding.

A few years ago I received a letter from a man who had been a soldier in Vietnam. He reported that he was able to receive *The Protestant Hour* on his small radio, even in the rice paddies. "Though I was not then a believer," he wrote, "that half hour provided the one sane voice in the midst of the carnage." He is not alone in his appreciation for the broadcast ministry of the church. Over mere words, shaped in the anguish of late-night preparation, the Holy Spirit hovers.

➤ ➤ ➤

John Vannorsdall is a former president of The Lutheran Theological Seminary at Philadelphia and a former preacher on The Protestant Hour.

HEARING

This Story Is Mine

by Karris Golden

*E*ver since I can remember, my maternal grandmother has told me stories—stories of her family, heritage, and life. My brother, Philip, and I grew up with Gramma Thomas and learned about her northern European heritage. She was always patient with us and had a special way of making us listen, and we wanted to hear the stories again and again.

As a person of color, these stories were essential in helping me shape my identity. Gramma told us stories about growing up during the Depression and her father's vow never to let his family go to bed hungry. Her face glowed with pride when she told us of her Swedish ancestors who were tailors to royalty. To express the importance of being independent, she often told us of her Irish grandmother who, upon arriving here from Ireland, struck out on her own after refusing an arranged marriage.

When Philip and I go places with Gramma, people stare at us. Many people have trouble accepting two very tall, brown-skinned, post-teenagers calling a White woman "Gramma."

When we were growing up, shocked people often asked
Gramma who we were talking to. When this would happen,
Gramma would laugh and say, "Well, don't they look like me?"

I often ask Gramma to tell me about riding the trains across
the United States when she was a little girl. Before starting the
story, she tells me many times, "You must've asked me to tell
you this a thousand times." I don't care, though, I tell her,
because I like the way she tells the story.

Finally she begins, and her eyes light up as she recalls visiting
an uncle in Cincinnati or traveling to the World's Fair. Telling
these stories will inevitably lead her into others, about her life
and about others in our family. Her face shines and her smile
almost brings tears to my eyes because this is the way she looks
when she is in church. I tell her she is beautiful, and she laughs.
When a reply is given, it is usually something like, "Oh, that's
just the Swede in me."

When Gramma tells me these stories, she probably doesn't
think she's giving me a sermon, but the significance of her message is priceless. Throughout my life, Gramma's storytelling has
been one of the defining influences in my faith and the way I
receive the gift of a preacher's message. God's presence between
us is undeniable.

My paternal grandparents spoke very little of their heritage,
most likely out of the painful history of their sharecropper
roots. I have never known prouder people. When they were
very young they migrated to northeast Iowa from Mississippi
and became successful Pentecostal evangelists. This had a powerful influence on me because it taught me to explore the world
outside the sphere of Lutheranism.

Grandpa Golden, a quiet man, was transformed each time he
stepped up to the pulpit. It was as if he were floating on a cloud,
with God's hand on his shoulder. His nervous stutter was gone,
replaced by his eloquent message. He no longer was aloof and
inconspicuous, but tall, animated, and imposing. Grandpa
would thrust his powerful hand toward the congregation, shak-

ing a Bible as if challenging us to reach inside ourselves for the strength to study the Word. As a small child, I watched him deliver his sermons, unsure of the full importance of his message, but aware of God's undeniable presence among us.

Grandma Golden is an immense woman—larger than life—in both size and personality. When she preached, Grandma was filled with the Holy Spirit, and it shook her body with the fury of a tornado. Her sermons scared and fascinated me because she stirred such strong emotion with her description of such a tremendous God.

As a pastor, Grandma always had a way of explaining things to me that otherwise seemed incomprehensible. For instance, I couldn't understand how God forgave so freely. She told me, "God sits in heaven and sees every sin you commit. But when you go to him and ask forgiveness, he puts all that sin in a capsule and throws it into space. Then he turns away and never looks back." Never? I couldn't believe it. How could God forgive so easily? "When you ask God to forgive you, and you mean it, that's it. Then he ain't studying it no more."

Also, after listening intently to her fire and brimstone sermons, I was frightened of the wrath of God, which seemed to be underscored by kinder messages in my Lutheran church. I developed a childish fear of being stricken blind by God in the middle of the night. I woke up often in the deepest dark of the night, sure God had finally sealed my fate. I would panic, sure I was blind. After weeks of this, I told Grandpa about my fear. He laughed and I got mad.

But Grandma always said God could do whatever he wanted. Grandpa smiled and said, "God tests our strength. This shows us how powerful our faith really is."

When I was eight years old, I mustered enough courage to ask Grandpa why one of his arms was twisted. He didn't give me an answer, only a sad smile. He walked over to the counter and picked up his hat and headed out to his garden. I looked at Grandma, and she looked at the floor and muttered, "Some

White boys beat him real bad when he was a kid. When he
refused to fight back, they beat him more." Her eyes filled with
tears, but they were gone when she looked up again.

Both sets of grandparents and the care they took to be a part
of my life is what makes me proud to be a biracial person. Their
stories from a favorite chair or from the pulpit gave me the
courage to embrace both the Black and White communities as
my own. Listening to their stories has taught me that another
person's testimony, while unique, can reveal our own personal
struggles and triumphs.

My grandparents and parents gave me the courage to hear
the stories of others. By letting these messages into my heart, I
am able to find my own spiritual path.

Now, as a fledgling adult, most of my mornings are spent in
my truck. I drive all over creation to get to school, work, *civilization.* Basically, this means I have a lot of time to myself. It
also means I have a lot of time to consider all of the things I can
do better.

No one is harder on me than I am. Lately, this has been especially true as I feel the push to become a grown-up. Recently I
found myself in a real funk. I was run-down, depressed, disor-
ganized—a complete emotional wreck. I found myself crying a
lot during my long country drives.

It happens to everyone, I guess, but that's really no consola-
tion when it's happening to me. While I drove, I would shut off
the radio and just look at the country around me. This, however, didn't help my mood much because in the winter Iowa is
barren and cold.

I thought about high school—the hotbed of regret. So many
things I wish I would have done and said. I was sure if I had made
different decisions then, everything would have turned better.

I loved going to church then. I went to different churches to
experience a variety of people and places. I loved sermons most
of all. It reminded me of the importance storytelling has always
had on both sides of my family. Whenever I heard the Word, I

was energized, and these personal messages and testimonies helped me shape a vision for my faith and for my life.

When I started college, I began to attend church rather sporadically. I went to daily chapel services, but I often found myself hugging my pillow on Sunday morning instead of going to church. I almost felt good about my decision to stay in bed because that's what everyone else was doing.

When people told me to become active in the congregation across the street from school, I was always ready with an excuse. In a month, I'd go to one or two services somewhere, but I was really too busy, studying too much, working too hard, to do much more beyond that. Gradually, I put more and more obstacles between myself and the church doors.

These decisions, of course, had an adverse effect on many areas of my life. One cannot survive merely on homilies and personal chats with God. This was why I found myself a junior in college, unable to find the direction I needed and the answers I was looking for; I had left my compass behind to wander around creation on my own.

I made an unconscious decision just to give up. I was at the point at which I wasn't concerned about success—I only did what I needed to do to get by. The whole time, I didn't know what the problem was. Something was missing, I just didn't know how simple it was to find.

Well, thank Jesus, he scooped me up, slapped my cheeks a few times, and revived my heart. On what I thought to be a routine Lutheran Youth Organization trip to Chicago, I heard the sermon that changed my life.

When the preacher stood before us, I realized what I needed was to return to God and hear God's voice through others. I had lost the story. As a Christian, I must be with others in community. I'd forgotten this when I was busy looking for quick fixes and any reason to excuse myself from this need. I was the ultra-independent college woman. I could do anything I wanted all by myself, on my own terms. I realized, however, that

what I couldn't do on my own was to fulfill the need to have the
Word satisfy my spirit and the testimony soothe my soul.

The preacher's personalization of the Word speaks to me. I
can't sit in the pew and just listen; my heart has to react. This is
the piece of the preacher's story that I can take and wrap
around my soul and make my own. The creeds and ritual are
our Lutheran tradition; the sermon is what makes it relevant in
our everyday lives. It is what we take home with us in our
hearts and minds.

During this life-changing sermon, the preacher told us of the
danger of doubting ourselves. He used Saul as his example. God
was ready to give Saul everything, but Saul, in a moment of
self-doubt, gave up his call. We were warned against taking such
a self-defeating, easy way out.

"The blessing is in the risk!" he shouted. How simple it was
for me to understand such a message. It had been both easy and
hard for me to ignore this challenge in the past.

Easy because I had isolated myself, unwilling to hear anyone's story. After that, I denied the effect listening to another
person's testimony had on me. I wouldn't allow anyone to rouse
me or make me recognize my gifts. I'd turned down the volume
on everything and everyone I didn't want to hear. It was as easy
as not visiting my grandparents as often or finding reasons not
to attend church regularly. If I'd done those things, I'd have
heard something to hold me accountable.

What was difficult was ignoring *my* voice because it was the
only one left, and it was the loudest. In giving up, I was shutting
that voice off, too. I was almost successful, until the preacher
made me realize what was at stake. Giving up wasn't easier, only
safer. I wouldn't have my heart set afire by someone's inspired
message if I simply avoided it. Yet at the same time, I was giving
up who I was, the part of me that gave me confidence. I was
giving up enjoying God's grace in community with others,
something I needed desperately to function in every part of my
life. I was turning in the gifts God had given me in exchange for
a bland life and nothing to challenge me.

It's been said that God takes care of fools and children. Now I am at the age at which it's getting harder to claim the latter case. Nonetheless, I was well taken care of that day. When I heard that sermon, a dam broke loose. The healing tears poured forth and dissolved the padding I'd surrounded myself with. I received what I certainly did not deserve—a second chance.

I felt as if the preacher was talking to me, though I surely was indistinguishable among the other faces. His words reached out to me and grabbed my hand, unwilling to let me lose myself to thickened skin and a hardened heart. To resign myself to a half-life—one in which I would give up and exist without using my gifts or accepting God's call—would mean to give up God's blessing. In giving up on myself, I'd pushed my chair away from God's table. This sermon was my invitation to return to the feast.

The story—not guilt or shame—brought me back. If I had waited for the pangs of remorse to do the same kind of number on me, I would have lost the strength to get out of bed long ago. The stories of others, because of their awesome power, have been the cornerstone of my faith and my life. The stories of my grandparents made me proud to be who I was; the stories of pastors and other preachers showed me all I could be.

In my foolishness, I thought there was a point at which a person could have their fill of sermons and go on alone. But the faith stories of others are like communion: They are essential to our oneness with Christ and each other, necessary for the spiritual cleansing and healing we all so desperately need.

For me, the worst thing about such sermons is that their deliverers never truly know that they have saved someone. This is because such a response is almost impossible to put into words. That day I realized that I have to hear the story. That is what I was missing.

➤ ➤ ➤

Karris Golden is president of the Lutheran Youth Organization of the Evangelical Lutheran Church in America and is a student at Wartburg College, Waverly, Iowa.

I Long to Speak Jesus

by Susan Briehl

The story of God entering human community, as told in the opening chapters of Luke's Gospel, has become for me a story of preaching in community. It is a series of stories, actually, in which the Word is carried first by one messenger, then another, into human ears, hearts, and lives. Nearest neighbors share the Word with one another until it spreads to all who will listen. Some receive the Word with disbelief or fear, others with wonder, joy, and faith. To all it brings the power to transform their lives by inviting them into God's future. In these stories I hear the story of my own community, as the Word is proclaimed and received in various ways and passed from one person to another. The circle grows ever wider, moving toward that day for which we all long when God's grace will embrace all peoples and mend the whole creation.

As Luke's narrative begins, a community has been created by the promise of God that is both word and deed: I will be your God; you will be my people. With this promise, the story of God and the story of the people became bound, for richer and for poorer, in sickness and in health, in life and in death. The faithful covenant community is represented by the gathering of the little

ones we meet in the beginning of Luke's orderly account:
Zechariah and Elizabeth, their neighbors and friends, Mary and
Joseph, the shepherds, Simeon the elder, Anna the prophet, and
all who wait with them for the coming of God's Messiah.

So it is where I live. The Holden Village community has been
created by the covenant of Baptism, when by water and the
Spirit individuals were knit into the body of Christ. The rhythm
of our life together finds its source in daily worship. As each day
gives way to night, we come together to welcome the light of
Christ into the deepening darkness. We sing our thanks for the
blessings of the day, pray for the needs of the world, and commit ourselves into God's keeping. On Sundays we gather
around the table of grace to be nourished by the presence of
Christ in his holy meal.

Yet this gathering of persons never has been present before,
nor will it remain. Every day some go and others arrive. Some
stay for a matter of days, others for a year or more. While familiarity, even intimacy, grows among the members, especially
during the winter months when the community is small and
isolated by deep snow, the seeker and the sojourner also are
always among us. They are living signs that this little gathering
is only part of the whole community of promise.

They come, so many, to this place apart to know God more
deeply, to be drawn by love nearer to the heart of holiness. They
long to face the doubts that nag and the skepticism that seeps
into their souls, to ask hard questions of the church, the nation,
their elders, their peers, themselves. They come hoping for an
experience of belonging they have not known elsewhere. They
want to strengthen their lives of justice-seeking and peacemak-
ing and to know more deeply their connection to the earth, its
beauty, and its suffering. Some come for healing, others for a
season of discernment or renewal. They come drawn by God's
promise to be present in this worshiping and working community. They come answering God's call to serve others.

I came to this community drawn by the same promise and
answering the same call—the invitation to be *theotokos,* God-

bearer. This Greek word is a title given by the early church to
Mary, the mother of our Lord. In her flesh she bore Jesus, God-
in-the-flesh. Not only at the birth of Jesus, but throughout her
life, Mary bore Christ to others by receiving the Word of God,
believing it, and acting upon it. This is the calling of every disciple who comes after Mary. It is our common baptismal
vocation.

The particular shape of my calling is to bear Christ into the
midst of the community through word spoken, water poured,
bread broken, and wine shared. Responding to this call is not
easy. Others teach me how to say yes with my whole life. Mary
responded to the invitation of the angel with such clarity that
it seems as if she had prepared for that moment for the length
of her days. From whom did Mary learn the words she
needed? From her ancestors in the faith, whose stories she
knew well.

"Here am I," Abraham said, when God came to test him. "Here
am I," Moses said, though he felt inadequate to the task ahead.
And when God called his name, young Samuel answered from
his bed, "Speak, for your servant is listening" (1 Samuel 3:10).

When, through the angel, God called Mary by name and
invited her to be *theotokos,* she said, "Here am I, the servant of
the Lord; let it be with me according to your word" (Luke
1:38). Her response was not original. It was faithful. In so
answering, Mary was in good company—the community of
the faithful who had gone before her. This is why I borrow
Mary's words. I say yes to the invitation to preach not because
I am without doubts or fear, but because I have learned from
the communion of saints so to answer and then to trust God's
mercy.

In fact, I often am terrified and tremble at the task, just as
Mary trembled at Gabriel's words. In Luke's story, immediately
after her encounter with Gabriel, Mary went with haste to her
kinswoman Elizabeth. She ran into the arms of her sister in the
faith. Within this embrace Mary heard God's call, not from an

angel, but from a member of her community of memory and hope. Each community I have been called to preach in has included an "Elizabeth," though their names are Carol, Daniel, Mary Elizabeth, and Dorothy. They have been honest and loving and wise enough to embrace me in times of fear and to confirm my calling as Word-bearer. They do for me what Elizabeth did for Mary. They take my attention away from myself and my anxieties by declaring the very presence of Christ within our embrace and at the heart of the community. In doing this, they become *theotokos* to me, speaking Jesus into my fearful heart.

I long to speak Jesus, God's enfleshed Word of healing and hope and peace. I want to speak Jesus into the hearts of those with whom I live. I want to speak with words they can hear, words that will slide under the locked doors of fearful, wary hearts; break through the walls of hardened hearts; and gently wrap the wounds of broken hearts. I long for them to speak Jesus into my heart, too. Do I tell God's story because I need the members of the community in which I live to have the Word in their hearts and on their lips for me? Perhaps.

What I do know is that though doubt is my nearly constant companion and though I feel inadequate and afraid, I would tremble more fiercely if I did not preach. For I believe, even in the midst of my unbelief, that only God can quicken the dead, mend with mercy what sin has torn asunder, and make of enemies friends. God's story alone, spoken to us in our hearts' native language in Christ Jesus, can bring authentic life into our living and our dying. So I tell the story. I preach.

Preaching has four phases for me: receiving, waiting, working, giving. Other preachers might speak of studying, reflecting, writing, and preaching. In my earliest years as a pastor, I became a mother, bringing two daughters to breath. Those experiences drew me more deeply into Luke's story of Mary's discipleship. She teaches us all something about being pregnant with the Word and what it means to receive such a gift, ponder its meaning, and labor to make it manifest to others.

The Holy Spirit will come upon you. Luke 1:35

By receiving I mean spending time studying and praying with
the texts. I study in community, a community of writers from
around the world and through the centuries who share the gifts
of their scholarship, insights, and struggles through books.
Moreover, I pray in the company of many others who that same
week are studying these same biblical texts, preparing to bear
the Word to those with whom they gather to worship.

Other communities are present, too, bringing gifts—the
communities for whom the biblical writers first wrote. I listen
with the children of Israel as Jeremiah speaks words of warning
to them before the exile and words of comfort to them when
they are weeping in a strange land. Paul's letters offer me
glimpses into the jealousies, disagreements, and generosity of
the communities with which he corresponded. The Gospels
invite me to enter as much as possible the diverse communities
within which the evangelists wrote.

I ask, how was that time like this time? That community like
the one in which I preach? How were their culture, economic
system, political situation, and religious climate like ours? How
were they different? The people to whom Luke wrote, or
Jeremiah, or Paul—what were their "golden calves"? What did
they fear that had the power to separate them from the love of
God? What "other gospels" tickled their "itching ears"? I seek to
know these communities as deeply as possible, to listen carefully to the words spoken to them as warning, judgment, comfort,
and grace, and to receive the gifts they offer.

Receiving is not work. It is an abundance of riches poured
out for me, for the sake of my community. And I am most
blessed among women to be so graced.

Mary remained with her about three months. Luke 1:56

Waiting marks the days before preaching when I am living in
multiple stories. The stories of my own community—stories of
struggle and joy, brokenness and healing—dwell beside the bib-

lical stories I have been studying. Side by side the stories unfold within me as I listen to National Public Radio, read weekly newsmagazines and journals, and attend to the prayers of my community each evening. I wait as the stories begin to connect with one another, or collide, or converse.

The questions that faced the biblical writers face me as well. I have to ask what our golden calves are. What threatens to enslave us or to separate us from God's love? What messages bewitch us as individuals, a community, a people? Where are the hungry waiting to be fed and the captives longing to be freed? When are the exiles welcomed home and the broken-hearted crowned with joy? How do the words spoken and written to those earlier communities bear to us the living Word that engages us and speaks in our time, to our condition, within our community? What is God's word of warning, judgment, healing, and peace to us this day?

While I wait, I live in community. We work and play together. Sometimes we feast, sometimes we fast, always we do the dishes and tend to the garbage. We hurt one another and seek forgiveness. We struggle to make decisions about our lives together. We try to be faithful to our common calling, to receive all who come to this community with the hospitality we first have received in Christ Jesus. At its best, all of this is part of our daily worship. Still, every evening we gather for prayer. In the midst of our ordinary days and deeds, a mystery is unfolding, unseen and unspoken. The Holy Spirit is brooding until the time comes when pencil must be put to paper or fingers to the keyboard.

The time came for her to deliver her child. Luke 2:6

Writing is work, difficult work. Each sermon has its own way with me. Some weeks the sermon takes shape gently. Phrases turn this way and that. Images float up like flowers. There is joy in this, but also danger. Too easily I can fall in love with my own language and begin to rely on my winsomeness rather than God's wisdom. Worse is the constant temptation to please the hearers, those with whom I must live so closely, rather than to speak the whole truth, the hard word, which so often must cut before it can cleanse and cure. I pray to remain faithful.

Other weeks the labor is long and difficult, wringing from me sweat and tears and all my energy. I grow anxious and angry with myself. I fear I will have nothing coherent to say, no word that is true, much less winsome. Why did I say yes? My community deserves more, needs more than I have to give. Here again "Elizabeth" speaks, saying it is the Holy Spirit and not I who brings the Word to life. And "Joseph," steadfast and faithful, reminds me that in community one never labors alone.

At other times the labor is fierce and fast. Water breaking. Words tumbling. Truth telling itself. The Word is willing itself to be born in the midst of community. I am not in control. Finally, exhilarated and exhausted, I catch my breath, wrap the Word in swaddling cloths, and prepare to bring it to the community.

They . . . present him to the Lord. Luke 2:22

As with writing, giving the sermon differs from week to week. The biblical texts shape the giving, as do the season of the liturgical year and the space in which we worship. When the room is small I can see every face, faces now familiar and filled with stories. I try to commit the words to memory in order to look more closely at the members of my community. Sometimes their faces reveal the toll of long days, early-morning shifts, heavy labor, late-night conversations, frustration with things that don't work, and an even deeper frustration with themselves. Sometimes their eyes are downcast or their minds distracted. Sometimes the demons are visible among us, the forces that rob of us life and shrink our worlds to the size of our own desires. Then there are times when I recognize in my community the faces of the shepherds who have left their work behind to see this wonderful thing that has happened among us, the coming of God into human community to bring peace.

Once in awhile I see Simeon, whose whole life has been shaped by leaning into God's promises and looking forward to God's future. His arms are bent, outstretched, ready to cradle the gift Mary bears to him. To Simeon the early church gave the title *theodokos,* God-receiver. His story reveals the miracle of preaching in community.

When he receives the Word that Mary bears, he gives the word that she must hear: "A sword will pierce your own soul too" (Luke 2:35). Her heart will be opened in the presence of God, revealing her inner thoughts. As with every disciple who comes after her, Mary needs to receive from another the Word that will both pierce her and bring her life. This happens, time and again, in my community. The one who bears the Word receives the Word from others, and those who receive become bearers of the Word. The gift is passed from one person to another, the circle growing ever wider.

Preaching in this community on Sundays always draws us to the table. With God's story and ours freshly spoken into our hearts, we stand in the company of the saints to praise and glorify God for all we have heard and seen. Even muted, disbelieving Zechariah joins the song. Then with arms bent and outstretched like Simeon's, we receive, in bread and wine, God's future now. As Luke will tell in a later story, the spoken Word makes our hearts burn, but it is in the breaking of the bread that our eyes are opened and Christ is made known to us. Here we become all that we receive—one bread, one body, blessed, broken, given for the life of the world. Then with Anna, who prayed night and day while watching for the redemption of her people, the community in which I live and preach is sent in peace to bear God's redeeming love, in word and deed, to the whole world.

➤ ➤ ➤

Susan Briehl serves as chaplain at Holden Village, Chelan, Washington, and is a noted preacher and pastor.

Come Over and Help Us

by Conrad M. Thompson

Come over and help us." This is a call that the apostle Paul heard one night in a vision. It's the same call that we hear today reverberating from across the seas and from distant lands and also echoing from the plains and cities, from hospital beds and retirement homes, from the young and the elderly, from believers in Christ, and from those whose faith may have dried up and weakened.

The call "Come over and help us" was loud and clear in the thousands of letters from *Lutheran Vespers* listeners: We need your message. Come over and help us—come into my home, come to my bedside. Come with a message of hope, healing, and encouragement. Come over and help us. Each broadcast was like casting a huge net of healing and love and forgiveness over an invisible, yet real audience—to the weak and the strong, the poor and the affluent, all seeking some affirmation, some hope to face the days ahead. Come over and help us.

To some people, *Lutheran Vespers* is a morning time of inspiration; to others, it is a closing devotion and benediction for the

Sabbath day. To some, it is a call to repent of sin and hear the word of forgiveness. To all, it is a challenge to live a more positive and victorious life in Christ. Each broadcast is really an extension of a congregation's ministry and witness of Christ. I thought of myself as an assistant pastor helping the congregations to build up the body of Christ, the church.

Radio broadcasting is one of the most economical ways to answer the call "Come over and help us." It spans all denominations and creeds. It touches the churched and the unchurched. It is no respecter of classes of people. It is listened to in the ghettos as well as in the mansions, in a quiet hospital room as well as in a car traveling the highways. It doesn't need cathedrals of stone or stained-glass windows or costly pews to gather its listeners. Those who have physical disabilities do not have to wrestle with traffic or crowds or be concerned about what to wear. A little transistor radio will carry the gospel direct to their homes and will meet their needs. A "lifer" in prison can have the same access to the gospel as the CEO of a large corporation. There are no walls separating us by age, denomination, nationality, or creed.

When *Lutheran Vespers* began its broadcast mission, there were very few religious broadcasts on the air. Television was still in the future. There were few easy-to-read Christian books on the market. People in the congregation generally had only one or two pastors to whom they could turn for edification, counseling, inspiration, and challenge. Today people have access to scores of different voices and books, each making a case for Christianity, some good and some bad. Through all of these changes, *Lutheran Vespers* has sought to be faithful to the gospel and to give to its listeners a consistent, dignified, Christ-centered message through both word and song. Week after week, letters testify to the power of God's word. If anyone ever doubts the Holy Spirit's working in and through *Lutheran Vespers,* let that person read the mail. There were letters from professors and students, clergy and parishioners, the churched and unchurched, believers and skeptics, the educated and not-so-educated—all in need of hearing and responding to the word of God.

A woman wrote, "I was just lying on the davenport listening to the sermon, and all of a sudden I jumped to my feet, raised my arms, and shouted, 'I'm a Christian! I'm a Christian!'" God had touched her heart, and she had responded. A Roman Catholic priest wrote and said, "On Sunday I get all emptied out spiritually serving my congregation. But Sunday evenings, listening to *Lutheran Vespers,* I get all filled up again. You are my pastor." I met a man one day who said that he was traveling late at night through a wooded area in northern Minnesota. He was listening to our broadcast. When the program was over, he said, he stopped his car, got out, knelt on the roadside beside the car, and claimed Jesus Christ as his Lord and Savior.

A young man wrote and said that when he and his wife listened to our program, their car became a sanctuary to worship and praise God. Some listened as they milked the cows at night. An editor of a large metropolitan newspaper, who was in intensive care with heart problems and whose countenance seemed hard and indifferent, demanded that his wife bring his radio so that he could listen to our broadcast. Another person told me that he was out fishing on a Sunday evening and tuned his radio to *Lutheran Vespers.* He turned up the volume, and soon a whole cluster of boats gathered and all quietly listened, even as they waited for the fish to bite! One day a friend, while walking along the beach, heard a familiar voice up ahead. He saw on the dock a radio broadcasting our program with not a soul in sight. A 107-year-old man had cassettes of all our broadcasts and insisted that his nurse let him listen to up to four each day, sometimes even at two in the morning.

There's power in the word of God. God speaks creatively through his word, whether it be from the pulpit, a tract, our daily devotions, or through the airwaves. The gospel is not ordinary news, it is good news. It is a message that the Holy Spirit writes on our hearts. To the casual observer, a broadcast may seem impersonal or even irrelevant. On the contrary, each broadcast paves a highway to human hearts and needs. The speaker's voice, in a very unique way, becomes the vehicle, the conveyer of the message of Christ. The listeners can't see you or look into your eyes. Yet the voice becomes the channel for communicating God's love. Even years later, people still tell me, "I know that voice."

The voice and the message establish confidence and trust. Many write for help in their walk with God and in their personal struggles. There is a boldness to tell an "invisible" pastor their troubles as well as share their spiritual experiences. The broadcasts become very personal, like a one-on-one conversation. I listened to their call "Come over and help us." As I prepared each broadcast, I visualized that vast audience, many seeking healing, forgiveness, love, and encouragement in their walk with God, some of them crying out from the depth of their souls, "Come over and help us." I discovered again and again the truth of what the writer of the book of Hebrews affirmed, that the "word of God was living and active and sharper than any two-edged sword." It would wing its way through the airwaves like the wind of the Spirit, and I could not know where it would touch and ignite a flame in some needy heart.

In 1982 when I retired as the speaker and director of *Lutheran Vespers,* my wife and I were asked to visit our radio listeners over a period of two years. What an exciting two years! We found it a rich and rewarding experience to visit with people who had been so loyal in praying for us and the broadcasts, and whose loyalty we found to be overwhelming. We were treated as good and dear friends, as if we had known each other personally for years. And we had, for the common bonding we had through our commitment to Christ our Lord and Savior was affirmed to us again and again. In fact, we enjoyed many of the same relationships that parish pastors experience with the people they serve.

Some shared with us their faith in Christ. Others shared their sorrows and heartaches and trials, and told us how much the broadcasts were helping them to cope with life. It seemed that in almost every home we visited we saw the closing benediction used on our broadcast hanging on the refrigerator or framed and posted in a prominent place for guests and family to see. In many homes we saw our printed sermons and cassettes. Some shared them with others, and many used them with their Bible study groups in their neighborhoods or congregations. In St. Cloud, Minnesota, we met a man who had most of the sermons I had preached over twelve years. He said he used them freely in his lay preaching in Catholic churches. One woman took a recording of each broadcast to a retirement community and played it for their Bible studies.

In one home a ninety-year-old couple invited us to see the exact place where they sat and listened to the broadcast. It was by a round table properly appointed and graced with the open Bible and hymnbook. Another woman, who lived alone, would dress up in her Sunday best, take her Bible and hymnbook, and reverently listen and sing the hymns. Her friends knew that this was a holy time for her and that she did not want to be disturbed.

In Long Beach, California, we were in an apartment building where a group of widows gathered each Sunday, played some table games, ate a potluck supper, and then listened to the songs and message of *Lutheran Vespers*. Often their times together were concluded with discussion and prayer. We were told that there were several such groups meeting each Sunday to share the broadcasts.

Many of our listeners were moved to support *Lutheran Vespers* not only with their prayers, but also with their monetary gifts. One such person was a farmer in Ohio. Years before we visited him, he and his parents, an unmarried sister, and five unmarried brothers had gathered each Sunday around their little radio to listen to our broadcast. When we met him, he was the sole survivor. His home was extremely humble, not even a telephone or television set. We replaced his small-print Bible with one with large print so he could read again. Because he was a lover of good sacred music, we furnished him with a cassette player and supplied him with tapes from our church college choirs. Occasionally, he would send a monetary gift, but when he sold his farm he endorsed the check and sent it to *Lutheran Vespers.* Unusual to be sure, but when combined with other larger and thousands of smaller gifts from friends, his gift allowed *Lutheran Vespers* to continue to broadcast the good news of salvation over many stations.

In our visits to hundreds of homes across the country, we always were met with enthusiasm and a hearty welcome. All seemed anxious to tell us of their spiritual journeys with the Lord and how much they had been blessed and inspired by the broadcasts. We were there to thank them for their prayers, their love, and their support of the program. These visits were among the highlights of our ministry.

One Sunday, after a very busy morning of preaching and an afternoon of visiting, we thought we should make one more call. We hesitated a little because the telephone operator said this person had an unlisted number. Usually we did not call on people unannounced. But we found the address anyway, we got to the house, and I rang the doorbell. Soon the curtain was pulled aside, and I heard a woman say, "It's Conrad Thompson." She had recognized me from pictures in our publications. Then we were invited in and introduced to this woman's mother, who was blind. With tears running down her cheeks, the mother said, "I knew that you were in this area, but I never thought you would call on us." She felt my face, then my wife Swanee's face, and welcomed us again and again. Here was a woman who didn't get out anymore, and *Lutheran Vespers* was her source of worship and praise each Sunday. When we left their house, we said to each other, "We are the most blessed by God in this visit with these saints of the Lord."

I state these examples to illustrate the close relationships that exist between the speaker and those who listen. One person wrote and said, "Believe me, dear pastor, we are here, neither nameless nor faceless, listening and hearing you . . . thousands of us . . . your radio family. And oh, how we need you . . . and bless you for your devotion to us and helping us to grow in God's word." Another wrote, "Who knows when something you say will touch us, . . . and when touched by the Word our lives will be changed. . . . All glory be to him, our Lord and Savior."

Yes, out there is a vast contingent of followers who not only listen and tell their friends to listen, but become prayer partners who help give the messages of *Lutheran Vespers* wings to answer the cry and call of many: "Come over and help us." I have had the privilege to be connected with *Lutheran Vespers* for forty-six of its fifty years. I thank God for the past and all of the fruits of faith, and I look forward to the future with great confidence and enthusiasm.

➤ ➤ ➤

Conrad M. Thompson is a former preacher for Lutheran Vespers *and a retired pastor of the Evangelical Lutheran Church in America.*

This Is Most Certainly True!

by William E. Diehl

I cannot remember as many as five sermons I have heard in all my life, including those I have preached myself." So said one of our Lutheran church's most popular and respected pastors at a recent conference I was attending. I was both shocked and relieved. Shocked to hear such an honest confession from a great communicator and relieved to know that my memory wasn't all that bad after all.

My wife, Judy, and I have been members of six Lutheran congregations and, over a period of more than forty years, have been served by nineteen pastors. The majority of them were good preachers, and we were nourished by them in both Word and Sacrament. I recall many times being moved by a sermon to the point of telling the pastor how great it was. Yet, in all honesty, I can scarcely remember a specific sermon of theirs from all those years.

As I reflect upon my journey of faith, I can identify certain stages of my spiritual growth with specific pastors, not by any one or two of their memorable sermons, but by general themes

that came through in their preaching. I cannot say if those
themes affected other listeners in the same way. It may be that
the soil was ready for me to receive a special word from God
and that I alone picked up those themes. All I know is that
those themes have greatly shaped my life.

"Our God is able!" is the most distant theme that I can recall.
Following the birth of our first two children, I returned to
church after a good five years of denying the existence of God.
The harrowing experiences of being in combat in World War II
caused me to reconsider my values and "to give church another
try," as I then put it. Leon Appel, the pastor of our little church
in Detroit, was a passionate preacher. He had no advanced academic degrees, and some might say that his vocabulary and
grammar needed improvement. But he preached with great
conviction. He did not lead us to believe that prayer was magic.
Prayer was no guarantee that our will would be done. But we
did need to pray with the certainty that the one who is the creator of all that exists is surely able to grant our requests. Before
Jesus restored sight to the two blind men, he asked, "Do you
believe that I am able to do this?" (Matthew 9:28). We never will
understand the mysteries of God or why some prayers are
answered while others seem not to be. Nevertheless, we come to
God with our cares and concerns with the certainty that "our
God is able!" That's what Appel preached, not in one specific,
dramatic sermon, but as a theme of his life.

Over and over again I heard those words: "Our God is able!"
They sustained me in those frightening days and nights at Ford
Hospital when Judy was so deathly sick that she didn't care to
live. Those words later led me into twice-daily intercessory
prayers for the sick and those in need, which have continued
without interruption for more than forty years. Those words
encouraged us to venture into things that ran completely
counter to my engineering-trained mind. Such as starting to
tithe when we could scarcely get by on a limited budget. Such as
signing papers that gave us full responsibility for sponsoring a

refugee family of five from East Germany. Acts that at first seemed irresponsible were undertaken with the certainty of those words which came from the Bible through the pulpit: "Our God is able!"

"Father, forgive them, for they know not what they do" were the words from one of the few specific sermons I do remember. It was on a Good Friday in the mid-1950s in an African American church in downtown Detroit. Three of us were the only Whites in the crowded worship service that day. What struck me in that sermon was that the preacher focused on the words "for they know not what they do." He accepted the forgiveness part as a given for all Christians. It was the part about hate so frequently arising out of ignorance that was burned into my mind that day. The preacher said Jesus calls us to forgiveness *and* understanding. It was the first time I heard Martin Luther King Jr. preach. Those were the days when few people had even heard of him. Since that day, I have heard many more of his sermons—some were written from prison and some were televised, including that magnificent one in front of the Lincoln Memorial before a crowd of hundreds of thousands. Always the "forgiveness plus understanding" theme was present.

Through the years my social-activist friends have become frustrated with my "hate the sin but love the sinner" philosophy. They hated Richard Nixon. They hate Jesse Helms. They hate the Ku Klux Klan. I cannot. Is one being holier than thou in adopting such a stance? Perhaps. But all I know is that a great preacher, Martin Luther King Jr., lived and died by those words: "Forgive them, for they know not what they do." It was a theme of his life.

It was the words of another African American preacher that propelled us into action in the civil rights years. The time was the early 1960s. The place was a Baptist church in an exclusive Main Line suburb of Philadelphia. John Perkins was the keynote speaker at a weekend conference on race relations, as we called it at that time. In his opening address he told of all the horrors going on in Mississippi—of the beatings, jailings, and lynchings of any Blacks—or Whites—who stood up for justice. His story was riveting, and I recall how sober we were when we went home to sleep that night. On the next day, Sunday, John was scheduled to preach. We arrived to find an all-White congregation, many of whom had been at the conference the previous day. There was the usual liturgy, hymn singing, a choir anthem, and prayers. Then John walked over to the pulpit. He intoned with a strong voice these stirring words:

> I hate, I despise your festivals, and I take no delight in your solemn assemblies. Even though you offer me your burnt offerings and grain offerings, I will not accept them; and the offerings of well-being of your fatted animals I will not look upon. Take away from me the noise of your songs; I will not listen to the melody of your harps (Amos 5:21-23).

He paused a moment, looked out at the congregation and continued in a slow and deliberate voice:

> But let justice roll down like waters, and righteousness like an ever-flowing stream (Amos 5:24).

And then he sat down. The congregation was shocked. Moments passed as they waited for him to stand and preach some more. But there was no more. It was a stunning sermon delivered by a poor Black preacher from Mississippi to a well-dressed White congregation in an exclusive suburb of Philadelphia.

After the worship service I heard some grumbling about the arrogance of Perkins to be so dramatic. But it sure had a telling effect on a few of us. When we stood around and asked, "Well, what can we do out here where there are no race problems," injustice seemed so far away.

But God supplied an answer within two weeks. A young African American Lutheran pastor whom I had known for several years was being transferred to the Lutheran offices in

Philadelphia. As soon as I learned about it, I phoned him and invited him and his family to our home when he was starting to look for a home. They accepted the offer, and during our meal I pointed out all the benefits our community offered him and his family. They were very interested. The shock came a few days later when I discovered that not a single real-estate agent would show him available properties.

A few phone calls to some friends in our congregation and neighboring churches soon brought into being the Upper Main Line Fair Housing Committee. Opposition to our efforts to ensure open housing quickly developed. A fellow member of my own church council submitted a motion that I should be removed from the council unless I resigned from the fair housing committee. Fortunately, other members of the council spoke on my behalf, but the vote was only slightly in my favor.

Our ecumenical fair housing committee launched educational programs in our congregations, pleading for justice. We met with real-estate agents, one by one, to appeal to their sense of justice. We ultimately prevailed when one courageous agent pledged to show all listings to any prospective buyer. In doing so he thanked us for persuading him do the right thing. Other agents soon announced the same policy.

In later years when I attended conferences with John Perkins, the theme was always the same—justice, justice, justice. Or, as he phrased it in secular terms, "Do right, White man, do right." Justice caused us later to support the movement for peace in Vietnam. We joined mass marches in our hometown, our state capital, and Washington, D.C., much to the consternation of my fellow executives at Bethlehem Steel. I became a member of Business Executives for Vietnam Peace. My involvement with that organization reached into the boardroom of Bethlehem Steel when our company was asked to become a corporate sponsor. The board declined, but I know it was the first time that our board of directors seriously discussed the Vietnam War during one of their meetings. It was God's call for justice, coming from the heart and soul of John Perkins, who brought a new theme into my life.

"Grace" is the theme that came to me from the preaching and writing of the beloved Joseph Sittler. I cannot remember a single sermon he preached (and he surely would chuckle about that), but the theme of grace came through in everything I heard him say and in the conversations we had. I have heard many sermons about grace from many excellent preachers, but the down-to-earth style of Joe Sittler has always moved me.

My life has been spent in a world of competition, goals, results, performance appraisals, merit raises, organizational effectiveness, and so forth. The world in which I operate daily identifies people by what they do, and values them by how well they do it. The word "grace" is absolutely foreign to the vocabulary of the world in which I have spent most of my life. The notion of a God who loves and accepts people without any merit of their own is absolutely contrary to my world in which acceptance has to be earned. The assurance of God's grace has come to me from many preachers, but if I had to identify one from whom it has come most convincingly, it would be Joseph Sittler. It was a theme of his life.

Grace helped me turn down a major promotion at a time when family needs were more important. Grace enabled me to challenge the silly perks and generally accepted customs that came along with being a senior manager at Bethlehem Steel— the "right" neighborhood in which to live, the special parking places, the executive dining room, the "right" friends to cultivate, the big cars, the fancy homes, the "right" newspapers to read, the "right" political party to support (guess which one?), the "right" sport to play (golf), the "right" schools and colleges for our children, and so forth. None of them was necessary for my own sense of worth. God's grace was sufficient. Grace enabled me to experience worldly success and failure with the same shrug of the shoulders.

Those who know me are aware that an important calling in my life has been to encourage all Christians to identify and carry out their daily life ministries in and to the world. This is one theme that, unfortunately, did not come to me from any of the pulpits of the various churches to which we belonged in the early years. On the contrary, the early messages about the role of the laity dealt with service *within* the congregation. Lay ministry occurred within the walls of the church building. Oh, there were those admonitions to "go into all the world," but the preachers really never knew how that would play out for members of the congregation, short of becoming a missionary. Nor did we.

It was a Quaker preacher who opened my eyes to the role of the Christian in daily life. I will never forget the first time I heard D. Elton Trueblood preach. "If you are a Christian, you are a minister," he began. "This proposition is basic to our understanding of the Christian movement. A nonministering Christian is a contradiction in terms," he said. Yes, of course, I thought. It was a new concept for me, yet it seemed so very logical that I wondered why it had never occurred to me before.

Fortunately, Trueblood was a prolific writer, and I immediately began to read his books. Starting in 1949 with *The Common Ventures of Life* (New York: Harper) and continuing for a quarter of a century, the books of D. Elton Trueblood gave me the biblical, theological, and practical insights to claim my own ministry in daily life within a church structure that didn't understand. Coming out of a Quaker background, Trueblood was not encumbered with a clerical church structure. He was not, however, anticlerical. He could write quite naturally about *all* Christians in their ministries.

Trueblood always came along with a new book for me as my growth in my own ministry needed nourishment. *Your Other Vocation* (New York: Harper) in 1952 gave me my first insight of daily work being a ministry. *The Company of the Committed* (New York: Harper) in 1961 spoke of the practical strategies for carrying out one's ministry, including the need for a support group of other Christians. *The Incendiary Fellowship* (New York: Harper) in 1967 put passion and total commitment to serve Jesus Christ into my heart. Through his Yokefellow movement I came to adopt the seven disciplines of prayer, scripture reading, regular worship, proportionate giving, ministry in daily work, service to others, and study. In *A Place to Stand* (New York: Harper & Row) in 1969 he gave a highly understandable biblical and theological perspective for the ministry of all Christians in daily life. I am sure the Holy Spirit was leading me along through the books and preaching of D. Elton Trueblood. It was he who encouraged my writing. During one of his stays in our home I said that I, trained as an engineer and engaged in selling steel, could not possibly write a book about the ministries of all Christians. "That's why you should do it," he said. I have since written seven books on ministry in daily life.

The theme of Elton Trueblood's life has always been the conviction that all Christians have been called into ministry in and to the world. That has become an important theme in my life also.

Looking back over the sermons and preachers who have made a difference in my life, it had to be their certainty that came through. They had something to say in which they passionately believed, and they wanted to share it with others. In the language of the street today, "They walked the talk." By the grace of God our paths intersected at the moment my faith was ready for another step forward.

What will be the next theme and who will preach it?

➤ ➤ ➤

William E. Diehl is a noted author on the subject of ministry in daily life and a former member of the Church Council of the Evangelical Lutheran Church in America.

Hearing One Another into Speech

by Barbara Lundblad

*I*t was fifteen years ago when they laid hands on me. I was serving as campus pastor at Lehman College in the Bronx alongside my work as pastor of Our Saviour's Atonement Lutheran Church. Campus ministry is never easy at a commuter college, but I was blessed with a wonderful colleague at the Newman Center, and I inherited two very active student groups—The Seekers Christian Fellowship and True Witnesses for Christ. At first, I wasn't sure this inheritance was a blessing! My theology, my political views, my worship style, and my religious history were all very different from my students'. They were primarily from Pentecostal traditions, and they taught me a great deal, including how to pray as I had seldom prayed before. When we prayed, we joined hands in a circle and soon the words began to flow—specific prayers for people in trouble, prayers of thanksgiving (always including the word "just," as in "I just want to thank you, Lord . . . "), and beneath the prayers, a gentle droning sound of "Alleluia. . . . Thank you, Jesus. . . .

Alleluia. . . . Yes, Lord. . . . " over and over under the other
words like the continuo in an orchestra.

During Advent the students asked me to preach at the
monthly meeting of all the religious clubs on campus. They
met the first Friday of each month in one of the college class-
rooms. The letters A, B, and C always were written on the black-
board to guide people giving testimonies—Audible, Brief, and
Christ-centered. I got to the room early, and some of the students asked me to join them in prayer. I put out my hand
expecting someone to stretch a hand toward mine, but instead
they asked me to sit in a chair. They formed a circle around me
and placed their hands on my head. Then they prayed. They
prayed that the word of the Lord would be spoken and heard in
that classroom. They prayed that the Spirit of the Lord would
rest upon me and upon all who gathered. "Alleluia. . . . Thank
you, Jesus" held up all the other words until the final amen
sounded. When they lifted up their hands, I still could feel their
weight on my head. I feel their hands every time I get up to
preach.

They taught me a great deal, those students. Prayer and the
laying on of hands are preludes to preaching. It would be a
good thing to do every Sunday morning—to gather a group of
lay people in the sacristy or in the center of the sanctuary to lay
their hands on the head of the preacher, to pray for the Spirit of
God to rest upon the one who preaches and upon all who listen. Preaching is never a solitary enterprise, never a monologue
even when only one person is speaking. Preaching is always a
conversation between preacher and listeners. This is true even
in traditions in which people are unlikely to respond aloud
with "Amen" or "Alleluia" or "Help her, Lord!"

I once worked with a very wise teacher named Philip
Swander who taught me to see those who listen as my preaching partners. Whenever we met he would set several empty
chairs around the room, then he'd ask, "Who is sitting in that
chair? Can you see her? What's troublesome to him? Where

will he be likely to nod in agreement? What will make her angry?" Facing those empty chairs, I would begin to read the scripture text, but I wouldn't get far! Phil would stop me, for it was clear to him that I wasn't listening to the text and I wasn't being attentive to my imaginary partners. I'd try again. Stop again. I never made it through one scripture reading without stopping.

Sermon as meeting place

In Exodus 3, Moses sees an unbelievable sight—a bush aflame, yet not burned up. He turns from the flocks he's tending and moves toward the bush. "When the LORD saw that [Moses] had turned aside to see, God called to him out of the bush" (3:4). That moment of turning aside made all the difference. It was in that moment that God spoke. Without such turning aside there would no preaching; there would be only words on a page or inside the preacher's head. The sermon is a meeting place between the text of Scripture and the text of the community.

The preacher must be attentive to both texts—the words of Scripture handed down over centuries, now written on the page, and the voices of the community, heard in the preacher's imagination or remembered from a text study group. The preacher also strains to hear those who will not be sitting in the sanctuary—the homeless man who stopped to ask for a subway token on Wednesday, the woman who hears the sermon from her bed in the nursing home, the Dominican grocer around the corner who speaks only a few words of English. As I try to hear the community text, I often write down the imagined responses of the community. Imagine: The text is Matthew 5:1-12 (the Beatitudes). John will laugh in disbelief—he lives in the real world and knows the meek don't inherit anything! Nancy will find it very hard to believe that those who mourn will be comforted any time soon. Chris will feel vindicated when he hears about prophets being persecuted for speaking out (his resolution about gay rights was just defeated by the city council).

I know that I cannot meet all these responses in one sermon, and if I try I may miss them all. But I will keep these voices in my head as I start to write. Only when *both* texts have been heard can the sermon begin to take shape. Then the preacher moves into the meeting place between the two texts. This is where the sermon takes shape, attentive to the words of Scripture and the voices of the community, the listeners' hands on the preacher's head. What word can interrupt the cynicism? What have these people seen that is like the image of a shoot growing from a stump in Isaiah 11? How can the preacher honor the honest questions spoken aloud or mouthed in silence? Attentive to both texts, the preacher stands up on Sunday morning. She feels the weight of many hands on her head. Then the preacher takes off her shoes and invites everyone in the sanctuary to do the same. Embarrassed and expectant, we all await the word of the Lord.

The Spirit is active in the meeting place

I feel the listeners' hands on my head even when I'm staring at a microphone in a recording studio. Radio preaching is an odd experience. For almost fifteen years I have preached to people I have never seen. *The Protestant Hour* is on at strange times—five or six o'clock in the morning in many areas, closer to prime time in the South. People listen in cars or in nursing homes; one man wrote that he listens while jogging. I try to see these listeners in my mind as they lie in bed or run along the lake. Thankfully, some have written to me over the years. These letters have sustained me and assured me that I wasn't speaking only to myself.

I remember Paul's letters especially—not the apostle, but a retired professor from a town north of Seattle. His letters were so moving that I saved them all, tied up in a little bundle in the bottom drawer of my desk. I asked his permission to include part of one letter in a speech some time back. He had written in response to a sermon about Jesus and the two disciples on the Emmaus road. My sermon was a retelling of that story—in fact, many of words were taken directly from Luke's Gospel. This is why I say the Spirit is at work in the meeting place—it was more than my particular words! The Spirit touched Paul as he heard this sermon and later when he read the text in a printed booklet. He wrote these words to me:

> Almost from the first paragraph I began to have trouble reading because tears kept blurring my eyes. When I came to the moment of recognition, I broke into uncontrollable sobbing. After I regained my composure, I came back to finish the story, and before I could read a whole sentence, the same thing happened again. I was very shaken, and put the book aside. What on earth was happening to me? The last tears I had shed had been during the '60s when I had been overwhelmed by the series of assassinations. My last sobs had been for my brother's death, when I was ten years old. I had often *wished* that I could cry, but I never could. After an hour of sitting and wondering, I went back to finish the story. This time I succeeded but with some difficulty, and at the end I once again sat weeping for several minutes. Since then, I have gone through the necessary motions of life, but my head and my heart are full of the same questions, endlessly repeated—what has happened; what is happening; what must I do?

In that same letter, Paul told me he had gone to church as a child, but stopped going all together when he grew older. As he finished college and then graduate school, he came to think of Jesus as a charismatic lunatic who had little to say to a professor of modern languages. But Jesus met him on the road to Emmaus. The Spirit moved Paul to turn aside to hear the words he had dismissed for years. Sometimes those of us who preach or listen Sunday after Sunday forget how *surprising* Jesus can be. Paul was caught off guard, open to being startled, uncertain but willing to start all over again. With every letter, he placed his hands on my head, praying for me and for himself. Ever since, I have tried hard to remember his questions, his dismissal of Jesus, his sobbing, and his astonishment at meeting Jesus as though for the first time.

Breaking silence and naming aloud

Since that long ago day when the students laid their hands on my
head, many other hands have joined them. Often, these hands
have been very tentative, sometimes afraid, not at all certain that
they have a place in any circle of prayer. More and more these
hands have commissioned me to break silence in the church, to
give voice to those who are seldom invited to speak.

I have felt women's hands on my head in a powerful way, not
only because I am a woman myself, but because women's voices
have been silenced over centuries in our Christian tradition. It
is not only that women could not be ordained, but that
women's stories often were discounted. Nelle Morton, fore-
mother feminist of faith, describes her experience listening to a
woman in a small group where she felt safe: "I have a strange
feeling you heard me before I started. You heard me to my own
story. *You heard me to my own speech.*"[1] Within the last ten
years, domestic violence has been named aloud in sermons.
Whenever I have named this pain in a sermon, a hand reaches
out to me. A woman from the congregation calls on Monday
and wants to meet me for lunch. A woman I've never met finds
me in the midst of a crowded conference. "I know you're very
busy," she says apologetically, "but could I talk to you for just a
few minutes?" Or a letter like this one comes in the mail following a radio sermon:

> . . . if there is any help for a mother and her six children, ages
> two through eighteen, please send her the contacts that she
> needs. . . . She was brought up in a Christian home and has been
> holding on for twenty years out of self-guilt. Her father and I
> have been praying and doing whatever we could do to help.

Naming aloud is part of our calling as preachers of God's living Word. There are hands on our heads that have not yet
found words to speak or prayers to utter; we are called to hear
one another into speech.

But naming aloud can be disruptive. We often prefer silence,
or we react defensively, insisting that "it isn't so" or claiming

that "it's someone else's fault" or scoffing that "it's not really so bad." Almost every time I have spoken about violence against women, one or two men have come up to me immediately after the closing hymn. "You know there are men who are beaten by their wives," one says. "And what about emotional abuse?" the other asks. I listen and I respond. Sometimes we connect, and other times our words pass without meeting. The statistics are almost always on "my side," but facts don't erase fear or anger.

The call to name aloud includes naming and talking through fear. What does racist fear sound like? The preacher must take this fear seriously, walk into it, speak the words aloud no matter how painful to move to the other side. As a White pastor, I must listen attentively to the fear of sisters and brothers of color, for fear surely crosses racial boundaries. How can I and this predominately White congregation hear the fear of African Americans? Can we hear the sixteen-year-old African American student who knows he cannot walk on the street with three other young Black men without risking police suspicion, even violent confrontation? How does he feel when he walks out the door?

As a pastor given the opportunity to preach and speak beyond the local congregation, I have heard and seen the great diversity of this church. I also know this diversity means that people don't always agree with what I say! I have become especially grateful for two things: signed letters and face-to-face conversations. These may sound like simple things, but they are not. I hope we keep trying them no matter how profoundly we disagree with one another across the church or within one congregation.

At the present time in the Evangelical Lutheran Church in America and in other churches, one of the scariest subjects of all is homosexuality. Gay men and lesbians are afraid—afraid of violence that threatens life and well-being; afraid of condemnation and ostracism from parents, coworkers, pastors, and congregations; afraid of teasing and name calling. Experience has taught that these fears are not imaginary, but painfully real.

Straight people are afraid—afraid of those who have long been labeled divergent or perverted, afraid that all the rules are changing, afraid that the Bible is being set aside, afraid of sexuality itself. These fears will not go away even if every preacher is silent. Unspoken fear often has the greatest power of all.

The hands of gay and lesbian people are on my head even as I feel the weight of others' fear. Shall I speak or remain silent? I have learned that a little goes a long way, both in affirmation and exasperation! When I have included gay men and lesbians along with others in calling the church to expand its boundaries, some have muttered, "Why does she always have to talk about gays?" (Similar to preaching one stewardship sermon, which elicits the reaction, "Why does she always talk about money?") But one little word of hope and acceptance can be received like water in the desert by gay men and lesbians who have heard only condemnation from the church. A few years ago, I preached at the closing worship at a synod assembly. I had included two sentences affirming the ministry of gay and lesbian people in our congregations. As I was getting ready to go to the airport, one of the ushers ran up to me with a note, words scribbled on a torn-off corner of the bulletin. The note said, "An offering is a gift of thanks to God, and I do thank God for my life. I also want to thank you for your words." It was signed, "A frightened gay man." I don't know his name, but I carried that scrap of paper in my wallet until my wallet was stolen a few months ago. The note is gone, but his hands are still on my head.

I never stand alone when I preach. I am surrounded by that great cloud of witnesses who have gone before me. The pages of Scripture pass on their words, and the walls of the sanctuary echo with their stories. The Spirit of God falls afresh upon me and those who lean forward to listen. It is one of the holiest moments I know, for God meets us as we turn aside together. A poet has given me words to say what I mean. Mary Oliver is writing about poems here, but I have changed the second word from "poems" to "sermons," for I hear her writing also about sermons: "For [sermons] are not words, after all, but fires for the cold, ropes let down to the lost, something as necessary as bread in the pockets of the hungry. Yes, indeed."[2]

Yes, indeed.

➤ ➤ ➤

Barbara Lundblad serves as pastor of Our Saviour's Atonement Lutheran Church in Manhattan, New York, and as a regular preacher for The Protestant Hour. *In the fall of 1997 she will become professor of homiletics at Union Theological Seminary in New York City.*

Endnotes

1. Nelle Morton, *The Journey Is Home* (Boston: Beacon Press, 1985), 205.
2. Mary Oliver, *A Poetry Handbook* (New York: Harcourt Brace & Company, 1994), 122.

I Love to Tell the Story

by Richard A. Jensen

*T*he story of the birth of *Lutheran Vespers* was told to me in this way. Pastor Harry Gregerson, pastor at East Side Lutheran Church in Sioux Falls, South Dakota, was driving home late one Sunday evening back in 1947. As he drove he listened to the radio. He heard the normal round of religious broadcasting and was distraught by what he heard. He was struck by the reality that there were few, if any, Lutheran voices to be heard in the medium of his day, which was radio. "It was like God was calling me through that radio program," Gregerson later said. Before long Gregerson had raised the funds to place a new program on a popular station in his area, WNAX in Yankton, South Dakota. The program aired on Sunday evenings, so Gregerson called his program *Lutheran Vespers*. Fifty years later we owe a great debt of gratitude to Pastor Gregerson for his visioning deed.

In the thirty-fourth year of *Lutheran Vespers'* existence, the call came to me. "Would you consider a call to be the director/speaker for *Lutheran Vespers*?" I knew before the ques-

tioner had finished the sentence that the answer was a
resounding, "Yes!" Up until that time I had been primarily a
teacher in the church. I had taught at Mekane Yesus Seminary
in Addis Ababa, Ethiopia, and at Dana College in Blair,
Nebraska. At the time the *Lutheran Vespers* call came to me, I
was teaching at Wartburg Theological Seminary in Dubuque,
Iowa. The cutting edge of my teaching had always been an
attempt to discern the intersection between the culture's questions and the church's attempt to address those questions.
When this call came inviting me to work directly at that intersection, it felt to me like the call of God's Spirit. This radio
ministry would be a medium through which I directly could
address the questions raised by human culture with the realities revealed for humankind through the pages of Holy
Scripture. I don't know that it ever dawned on me that I
should say anything but yes to this call. As the old hymn by
Katherine Hankey sings it, "I love to tell the story of Jesus and
his love." To be invited to tell that story nationwide and weekly
was a challenge I could not refuse.

"Yes," however, is easier said than done. The task of preparing a weekly message for a wonderfully far-flung audience was
an incredible challenge to my mind and my imagination. It is
one thing to preach weekly to a congregation one knows. It is
quite another thing to preach to a radio congregation that one
knows hardly at all. I believed that the only reality that could
possibly connect me to this audience was God's word.
Therefore, I began my work at *Lutheran Vespers* by preaching
through the Gospel of Matthew text by text, week by week.
Having preached my way through Matthew, I determined to
open up my sermons a bit more to the world of culture that I
loved. Therefore, the first week after completing my preaching
on Matthew, I preached a sermon on the popular novel and
television series *The Thorn Birds*. We received more requests for
that sermon than for any other sermon that I had preached on
Lutheran Vespers up until that time.

In the years that followed I kept close in touch with the artists of our culture. I did this because I believed (and I still believe!) that our artists are astute analysts of the human condition. I preached sermons over those years on everything from John Updike stories to popular musicals such as *Phantom of the Opera* and *Les Misérables*. I worked to bring biblical insights to bear on the questions raised by our culture's artists. The audience response was deeply gratifying. These stories from the world of cultural artists proved to be useful tools for gospel proclamation.

Stories from our culture worked. Why? I worked hard to come up with an answer to that question. The path of discovery led me into the world of human communication. I came to understand that there have been three basic periods of human communication. The first era of human communication we call "oral." Our earliest ancestors learned the world of their culture through the words of other people. They learned through their ears. The primary teachers in this oral culture were the storytellers. These storytellers not only told stories, but they thought in stories. Most of our Bible comes to us in the form of stories.

The second era of human communication comes with the invention of the phonetic alphabet in about 700 B.C. We can label this "literate culture." Learning took place by reading. Eyes replaced ears as the primary sense used in learning. Author Marshall McLuhan once said that Western civilization gave us an eye for an ear. Learning with the eye is primarily a linear experience. This shift from oral culture to literate culture took place over a period of almost two thousand years. It was only with the invention of the printing press during the 1450s that print could be made available to the masses and eyes could replace ears as the normal sense through which learning took place. Learning through the eye is characterized by linearity and order. We read words on a page that are linear. Everything is in order. Ordered explanation begins to replace storytelling as the human coin of knowledge.

The third era in human communication is the world of electronic communication, which began in the nineteenth century with the invention of telephone and telegraph and has picked up incredible speed in the twentieth century with the inventions of movies, radio, television, computer, the World Wide Web, and so forth. We can call this postliterate culture. It is instructive to compare television with reading. In reading we use only our eyes. In watching television we use our eyes and our ears. Our whole body, McLuhan argued, is engaged physically with the manifold electronic information communicated to our senses through television.

Electronic communication has brought us into a new era of learning. Experts often call this new world a "secondarily oral" world. In the oral world ears were the primary sense of learning. The literate world shifted us from ear to eye. This is often called the world of silent print. The electronic age has brought our ears back into play again. The communication world is no longer silent. Ears are engaged as they were in oral culture. The electronic culture is like the oral culture (hence, "secondarily oral") because both of them engage the ear.

All of this has tremendous implications for preaching. Preaching in the last half of the twentieth century still is shaped largely by the literate world of the eye. Textbooks for preachers have been sculpted in a literate vein. Ideas dominate such teaching of preaching. The only thing I ever learned about preaching in seminary was that it was about ideas. Sermons convey ideas, usually three of them. Sermons explain things. Sermons explain the Bible.

I came to the task of preaching on *Lutheran Vespers* shaped primarily by this literate approach to preaching. Once I realized, however, that human communication patterns were shifting from a literate to a postliterate world, I knew that my preaching, too, must change. Literate forms of preaching did not fit radio! Radio reached people's ears. Radio is an oral medium. I realized that I needed to move my preaching to a postliterate mode. And what would that be? It would be what was once-upon-a-time in a world of oral communication. Preaching would be shaped for ears. In the world of the ear, in the world of oral communication, storytelling was the dominant mode of communication. I would need to make a distinct shift in my preaching. I would need to learn to be more of a storyteller. Like the storytellers of old, I would need to learn to "think in stories" as I prepared my sermons.[1]

My conviction became strong. Preaching to this generation—preaching to a postliterate generation—would involve a great deal of storytelling. But what stories was I to tell? I already was familiar with the stories told and sung and painted by our artists. That was one source of stories for preaching. My own autobiography was another source of stories. Stories of other people, whether individuals or communities of faith, also would be an important source of stories for my preaching. Stories also could be created by me as stories that helped bring the gospel alive. That's what Jesus did. He told stories of invented fiction. Garrison Keillor notes that fiction was the art of choice there at the inception of the gospel. Fiction was the only art form that Jesus used to communicate his message. Our own fiction told in the interest of the gospel puts us in line with a host of Christian storytellers over the ages dating back to Jesus himself.

Slowly I learned to teach myself how to think in stories. In my sermons I told stories of myself, stories of other people, stories from our artists, and stories I invented. I told these stories as metaphors of participation rather than as metaphors of illustration. Metaphors of illustration are stories told to illustrate the meaning of a point. Metaphors of participation are told to create meaning in and through their telling. That's what Jesus did. He told stories that were revelatory in and of themselves.

It soon became clear to me, however, that the greatest source of stories for the telling in preaching was the Bible. And so I began to tell Bible stories. Time and again the biblical stories themselves provided the substance of my preaching. One summer I preached some of these biblical story sermons in a summer camp for adults. The theme of the week was basic Lutheran doctrine. I took bedrock Lutheran teachings such as grace alone and faith alone and told Bible stories that supported these Lutheran themes. At the end of the week I asked a couple of retired schoolteachers what they thought of my biblical storytelling sermons. Frankly, I expected them to tell me that they didn't need to hear these Bible stories because they already knew them. But that's not what they said. What they said was, "We've never heard them whole before." They had heard preachers explain these stories and give points about these stories, but they never had heard the stories in their fullness. In our world of biblical illiteracy on the way to the twenty-first century, therefore, I would like to hold up the possibility of telling more Bible stories in our preaching as a crucial way of shaping preaching for our time. Telling biblical stories is almost always more important than the points made about the stories.

My own interest in biblical storytelling has coincided with a time in biblical studies when the Bible is being studied from the point of view of its narrative quality. In my seminary training I learned that the Gospels were a patchwork of bits and pieces with no particular relationship with any other passages in a given book. Our whole method of preaching in the church is based on this approach. We preach from the lectionary. The lectionary appoints a few verses from each Gospel per week. Preachers study these brief verses and preach a sermon based upon them.

Narrative students of the Bible, however, are now claiming that the Gospels have a story flow to them. The paragraphs in Matthew, Mark, or Luke are not just isolated snippets of information. They are part of a total story. Narrative students of the Bible ask us to see any given paragraph in the Gospels in the light of other paragraphs and overarching themes in that Gospel. This gives a whole new outlook to preaching on the

paragraphs in the Gospels. We know how to dissect these paragraphs in the search for ideas to communicate. What we need
to learn how to do for our time is to see how these paragraphs
get their fuller meaning from other paragraphs, from other
parts of the Gospel story. Sermons have traditionally taken
these paragraphs in isolation and dissected them for their ideas.
We also need to learn how to see these Gospel paragraphs in
light of other aspects of each Gospel. Preaching in this vein
would be a kind of biblical storytelling. We tell two or more
stories from Mark's Gospel, for example, in order to paint a
more complete picture of Mark's picture of Jesus.[2]

We live in a world that is increasingly postliterate. Electronic
communication has created a new way of being engaged with
the vital realities of life. One of the things preachers can do to
reach this postliterate generation is to learn to "think in stories"
as weekly sermons are created. Our world is also often referred
to as a postmodern world. The modern world, as scholars use
the term, began about the time of the Reformation. Various
commentators on the nature of the postmodern world say the
following kinds of things:

1. In the modern world humans were very optimistic about creating a better world for tomorrow. In the postmodern world
   humans have become quite pessimistic about their human
   future.
2. In the modern world truth was understood to be purely
   rational and quite certain. In the postmodern world truth is
   understood to come from many sources, not just our minds.
   There are many paths to knowledge.
3. In the modern world it was believed that knowledge was
   objective. The truth of any given thing, that is, could be proved
   true or false by using scientific data. The postmodern world
   believes that knowledge is subjectively shaped. Each human
   community understands knowledge in a different way.
4. The modern world believed in the possibility of a single, universal worldview. In the postmodern world we are understood
   to live in a "multiverse" of many valid worldviews.

These postmodern assumptions pose a serious problem for the Christian church as we seek to communicate our "universal message." It is difficult to make claims for a single, universal truth in a world that believes there to be a pluralism of truths, for example. In the past the Christian church has often simply confronted the world with its truthful ideas. Ideas have been our way of communicating with the world. But the world now believes that many different ideas can be true. Proclaiming the truth of our ideas in our preaching and in our address to our world won't get us very far with postmodern people. But we can tell stories! Stories address human beings at many levels of their being. Stories, that is, are not addressed solely to human thinking capacity. Think of the Christmas and Easter stories, for example. These stories still can be told in all their power and mystery to postmodern people. We ought not reduce these multifaceted stories to a couple of ideas! Tell the story. Let the Spirit work with the story. Storytelling is a vital means for reaching out to people in a postmodern world.

Storytelling is also an effective means of communication with that specific group of postmodern people known as Generation X. This is the designation of that generation of people who were born roughly from 1964 to 1974. There is not space here to completely characterize this generation whose favorite color is black, whose motto is "whatever," whose lives have been ruined by divorce, and whose philosophy of life is that of an oppressed generation desperately seeking to survive.

In his excellent book on Generation X, titled *Jesus for a New Generation* (Downers Grove, Ill.: InterVarsity Press, 1995), Kevin Graham Ford proposes three strategies for reaching out with the gospel. First, we must present this generation with a picture of a faith that works itself out in public. Lutherans would call this the priesthood of all believers. Ford is convinced that Generation X will be impressed only with a way of life that works for the good of others and for the good of the cosmic environment.

Second, we only can reach the members of Generation X if we are willing to practice incarnational evangelism in which we choose to relate to members of this generation over time. Ford calls this process evangelism.

Third, our evangelism with Generation X ought to be a narrative evangelism. Ford sees narrative evangelism—that is, storytelling evangelism—as a "new-old" approach. Storytelling of the gospel is new; this generation has not seen this approach before. At the same time, Ford argues, this form of evangelism is old; it is the same approach as that used by Jesus and the early evangelists. Ford is convinced that storytelling evangelism is the only evangelism that will speak to a media-saturated, story-hungry generation. This generation wants the feelings and the action of a story. Ford puts it very strongly: "In fact the story of Jesus Christ seems custom-designed to give Xers a story to identify with . . . "(p. 228).[3]

"I love to tell the story." I really do! That's why I quickly responded to the call to serve *Lutheran Vespers* many years ago. I love to tell the story because I believe that this kind of "thinking in story" in our witness to our world is very effective in a postliterate age. Furthermore, I believe that storytelling is effective in our postmodern world where rational ideas no longer fill the void in the lives of people. Story preserves mystery. Stories open up the avenues for the work of the Holy Spirit. Finally, I am becoming convinced by analysts of Generation X that storytelling is the most effective means we have of reaching out to many young people in our world today.

Let us then become storytellers for Christ. Tell the story. Trust that the Holy Spirit will use your words to blow God's breath of life into the ears and on down into the hearts of postliterate, postmodern, and Generation X hearers. I love to tell the story!

➤ ➤ ➤

Richard A. Jensen serves as professor of homiletics at Lutheran School of *logy at Chicago and is a former preacher for* Lutheran Vespers.

Endnotes

1. See Richard A. Jensen, *Thinking in Story, Preaching in a Post-Literate Age* (Lima, Ohio: CSS Publishing Co., 1993) for a full description of this movement in preaching for the twenty-first century.

2. For preaching help of this nature I refer you to Richard A. Jensen, *Preaching Mark's Gospel: A Narrative Approach* (Lima, Ohio: CSS Publishing Co., 1996); *Preaching Luke's Gospel: A Narrative Approach* (Lima, Ohio: CSS Publishing Co., 1997); and *Preaching Matthew's Gospel: A Narrative Approach* (Lima, Ohio: CSS Publishing Co., 1998).

3. For an excellent study of Generation X and a Christian response to this generation, see Kevin Graham Ford with Jim Denney, *Jesus for a New Generation* (Downers Grove, Ill.: InterVarsity Press, 1995).

God Speaks to Doubters, Too

by Barbara Berry-Bailey

*J*ournal entry, November 25, 1996: It is 6:20 in the morning. After an invigorating walk-run with my fat-busting buddies and a healthy send-off breakfast with my husband, John, I have exactly seventy minutes of silence before I awaken my three-year-old daughter, Cynthia. She will be bright-eyed, cheerful, and totally obedient—not! At 7:30 the morning madness begins: wash, help dress, coax, prepare hot breakfast, answer questions about God and the universe in a manner that a preschooler can understand, comb hair, coax, inspect brushed teeth, head out for Montessori school and the church office for even more madness (but at least that's madness for Jesus' sake).

As I caress my oversized mug of French roast coffee with cinnamon, I realize that I really ought to give up this stuff, but on a pastor's salary, what other over-the-counter drug can I buy to give me the kick I need to get through the day (pastors' Bible study, answering phone calls, three hospital visits in hospitals on opposite ends of town, three private communions, cooking dinner, committee meetings, husband/wife together-before-we're-too-crabby-and-exhausted time)? On the radio, I hear a story on the local public radio station of an all-consuming predawn blaze in which no one was killed, but in which three homes were totally destroyed. I think, "These people's lives will never be the same." On the television set of my mind, I can see the "film at eleven" yellow and red flames on the black early-morning sky. The smell of coffee jolts me back. I turn off the coffeepot and check the stove. I left the burners on all day yesterday. You just can't see the flames on an electric stove. And who pays attention to the surface-unit light? Obviously, not me. But I really do have to be more careful about turning off electrical appliances.

It is so quiet, despite being in the city and just one block away from Lincoln Drive, a major rush-hour traffic artery. I can hear the kitchen clock ticking. Funny, this is the only time of day I can ever hear that clock tick. I love this sound of silence. I had to age twenty-six years to understand what Paul Simon was singing about. I'll have to get myself ready soon before starting my Cynthia routine.

Seventy minutes of silence is just not enough, which is probably why I began writing my sermons on Fridays at four o'clock in the morning. Since Friday is my day off, I don't have to worry about being tired later in the day. Cynthia will be at school. I can just turn off the phone and nap if I'm around the house. (I have been known to take a nap in the shopping mall parking lot. It started when I was pregnant with Cynthia and just could not get through the long days with hospital visits and night meetings. So I would take naps in the hospital parking garage. Who even knew?)

It didn't always start out with me writing my sermons at four o'clock in the morning. I used to take an entire month to write just one, during my internship. My supervising pastor would plan the preaching schedule six months in advance. So I would select my text six months ahead and spend the better part of each month typing and storing, editing and moving text, grammar and spell checking for that perfect sermon that I would preach once a month. I recalled something a professorial candidate for homiletics once said when asked about ideas for sermon illustration. He said, "You have hundreds of illustrations that occur in your life on a daily basis. What you need is the serenity to discern how the Spirit is using you and how God is acting in each instant of each day."

Wow! Each instant, huh? Well, in my life, if I don't write it down it is gone. So I began what I called "coffee-can homiletics." After doing all the exegetical work, translation (yes, Hebrew or Greek), literary criticism, form criticism, and historical criticism, I then would be in search of "the illustration." As I encountered interesting, amusing, or even disturbing situations in the course of the month, I would write them down and toss them in an empty two-and-one-half-pound Maxwell House coffee can (I fantasized about delivering sermons that were good to the last . . .). From time to time throughout the month I would go through jots, read and reflect, journal, and allow the sermon to perk, so to speak.

Then the week before the sermon was to be preached, I would prepare the weekly congregational Bible study, absorb comments from the discussion, and a day later begin writing the sermon. The actual writing took a few days from start to finish, editing all along the way. Finally, voila! At that time, I believed the actual delivery was only secondary. It was for me because I had spent seventeen years in public radio and television. Delivery was not a weakness. Then during an assignment at an ecumenical organization, I heard a Pentecostal colleague refer to the actual moment of preaching—the delivery of the well-crafted sermon as being the moment of the "anointing of the Spirit." I asked, "What about when you write it?"

She said, "No, no, you're not anointed until you open your mouth and it comes out." Later I realized why she felt that way—she didn't write her sermons. She didn't even preach from notes or an outline. The fire of the Holy Spirit would fall upon her, and she then would begin to speak the word of the Lord.

This troubled me, this business of the Holy Spirit being present only when you stood in the pulpit. To think that all that prepulpit work was not considered to be spiritual. What was it then? It was then that I began to wrestle with the concept of the preaching moment.

For me the preaching moment is not only when I stand in the pulpit; for me the preaching moment begins even before beginning to write the sermon. The preaching moment begins in Bible study. Once I have done the research and presented who, what, when, where, why, and how, I hear the stories of struggle from my members: how Elyn suffers humiliation and is branded "foolish" by her coworkers because she chooses to use her vacation time to attend a Global Mission event rather than going to the Bahamas. I hear how my seniors feel trapped in a Serlingesque cyberworld in which they cannot communicate. How Sharon at midlife has not yet found her career niche and is chided by her friends that she has missed the boat. Sometimes, usually at council meetings but also through "anonymous" phone calls (I know every voice in my congregation), I learn of some evil plot to expose another member's "sin."

The preaching moment is an ongoing process, not a fixed point in time. As their pastor, I need to interpret how one sentence addresses their setting in life in the Christian community and how that impacts their setting in life in the secular community.

The recounting of members' struggles and joys, knowing the ravenous wolves who call themselves sheep but who feed on the misfortune of other sheep, seeing one church member's inhumanity with regard to another church member—these make up the volatile fuel in which I am doused. In the light of day, I walk around drenched, processing, searching, unsuccessfully trying to assemble all the pieces. It is only in predawn stillness at four o'clock that the fire of the Holy Spirit without fail ignites into a blaze as I sit at my computer and it all rushes from my soul to my fingertips.

I have tried writing sermons at two o'clock on Friday afternoons. I stare at the screen until I fall asleep, resting my head on the space bar and creating twelve pages of absolutely nothing. Once or twice I have actually written a sermon or two during daylight hours, only to awaken fourteen hours later and rewrite them. And they become entirely different—so much so that I even have used different texts. Maybe it is because I was born on December 25, but for preaching purposes, the Holy Spirit, like jolly old St. Nick, seems to visit me only when everyone is asleep. (By the way, as I write this, what time do you think it is now?)

So there I sit "on fire" and still burning until I stand in the pulpit. The pulpit event is another part of the process in the never-ending circle of the preaching moment. While on fire I begin, "Grace to you and peace from God our Father and the Lord Jesus Christ." With every illustrative story, exhortation, admonition, proclamation, gesture, inflection, the roaring flames die down to quenched embers. I see Terence smile, I see satisfaction in the eyes of Elyn, I see my seniors nod their heads in agreement, I see the wolves morph back into sheep and later approach the altar rail with their hands extended to meet the Christ whom they again may misunderstand and harm in his name. I hope, that like that predawn blaze reported in the news, "When will their hearts be changed?" I want them to be unharmed, but I want them to tell it on the mountain that because of the Word, "Our lives never will be the same." I believe that in time it will happen. I wonder, "Will I live to see it happen?" Or, like Moses, will I sow proclamation and prophecy and leave the reaping to another?

Therefore, I no longer understand the delivery as secondary or only an ancillary activity. The pulpit serves as the font in which I immerse in the water that cools, not extinguishes, the

predawn blaze. In the preaching moment I am made new—new
to go through the process again and be renewed again with eyes
that see the same pericope three years later in an entirely different way. In my earlier days as a pastor, I would be so exhausted
by the process that I would have to take a nap every Sunday
afternoon.

In urban congregations there is oftentimes a situation in
which children have been baptized into membership and the
parents remain unchurched. The kids are introduced to the
community of faith through vacation Bible school or summer
day camp. I recently had a preaching challenge, or should I say
that I had a hard time getting the fire started? The father of a
youth member died. He had not confessed Jesus Christ as Lord,
he had not been comfortable in worship "in any church," and
he had not wanted to attend his own daughter's Baptism. Yet
his wife wanted to have his funeral in our church, the same
place in which both daughters had been baptized and one was
to be confirmed. What do I say about a man who refuses to
worship the King?

Knowing that most of the people in attendance would not be
members of any Lutheran church and maybe even would be
unchurched, I wrote the following sermon at four o'clock in the
morning on the day of his funeral:

"Grace to you and peace from God our Father and the Lord
Jesus Christ.

"Many people spend their entire lives questioning and seeking the purpose of life. Paul Smith (not his real name) was one
of those people. Ironically, it is in death that all questions are
answered; and for those who are left here to mourn his death,
you can be comforted with the fact that neither death nor life,
nor things to come nor things past can separate him from the
love of God. Because with all our faults and shortcomings we
are all children of God.

"Not things past nor things to come. Things past. As we sit
here, pictures of Paul in various community and family settings

are probably racing through your minds. You may see him smile or laugh, you see him busily carrying out his responsibilities in the community, you see him intensely striving to be an effective parent and in his own way seeking the Lord where the Lord may be found. Though he may not have done it in the conventional manner, he did wrestle with issues of good and evil. He did confront issues of right and wrong, love and hate, and worked very diligently, maybe sometimes to a fault, to bring about shalom—not just peace but wholeness, especially wholeness of life for people in his community.

"And to be snatched from life without warning leaves unanswered questions in the minds of all his loved ones, those who *do* confess Jesus Christ as Lord as well as those who pray to some other deity.

"As Christians, we believe and teach that all who call on the name of the Lord will be saved. And a relationship with God is a four-way intersection really. If you consider that when we make the sign of the cross, we communicate that intersection— the relationship is vertical between God and me, but it is also horizontal between us. Most often our vertical relationship guides our horizontal; that is, a person's relationship with God guides how they relate to other people. But sometimes it works the other way around—God working in and through other people can drive a person to seek the Lord where the Lord may be found.

"And that very act of seeking, whether all your friends, family, and coworkers know, constitutes faith. Looking for something means that you believe it is there.

"As I stand here I am reminded of a man I knew when I lived in Ohio. The building in which I worked was a modern one-story structure with glass windows halfway up the wall for the entire length of the building. As I walked by the window I looked out to see a tornado touch down, and the building I was in was in its path. As I went screaming down the hall warning my coworkers, I realized that one of our staff members had just left the building and was walking across campus to another building. Judging from the time he left and the distance he was walking, he would not be able to get to where he was going before the twister reached us. Horace (not his real name) was an avowed atheist. We all knew that because he never ceased to remind us. As we all huddled together in a tiny closet in the southwest corner and listened to the roaring wind, we silently wept for Horace.

"Though it seemed like an hour, minutes later we opened the door to find the roof torn off in several sections, though it stayed over the closet in which we sought safety. Not a pane of glass was left in the window frames, and shattered glass was strewn everywhere. Electrical wires hung from the ceiling, and we were careful not to touch anything. People went to their offices to see what they could salvage. Some ran outside and let out bone-chilling shrieks upon seeing their cars turned upside down with the windshields sucked out. In the middle of all the devastation and loss, I heard someone shout, 'Horace!'

"We ran as he was staggering through a broken glass door.

"He looked confused, but he was unharmed. There was no way to make him something hot to drink. Someone had a thermos of coffee and dug through piles of torn, rain-soaked drywall to find it. The one blanket in the entire building was covered with glass and debris. We used our coats that were in a closet to cover him up. We didn't know when help would arrive because the phones were out. Because our campus was miles away from the city, we didn't even know if anyone knew we needed help.

"Horace came around finally and was conversant. And someone awkwardly blurted out how we all thought he had been killed. 'What did you do?' he was asked.

"He said, 'When I looked in the distance and saw that big dirt funnel coming, I feared for my life and prayed to God.'

"No one laughed. There was silence for a very long time. The silence was interrupted by the sound of Horace's voice continuing his account of how he jumped into a ditch and climbed into a drainage pipe.

"'I guess I've always known there was something greater than human beings,' he said. 'I guess I never had the opportunity really to think about it until I saw that tornado.'

"For many people, staring death in the face is what jars them from sleep into the realization that there is an almighty creator. For those who sit here now and wrestle with questions of faith, for those who wonder about God and how God acts in your lives, I urge you to continue wrestling because the power of the Holy Spirit is stronger than your doubts.

"If you seek a place to help you with your wrestling match and the exploration of the holy, I invite you here because as human beings, we all fall short of perfection, but that is the nature of a Christian—one who is in need of forgiveness and the strength of the community.

"Paul's search has come to an end. Paul's struggle is over. Paul has found his answers. Have you found your answers?"

➤ ➤ ➤

Barbara Berry-Bailey, a dynamic African American preacher, serves as pastor of Trinity Lutheran Church in Philadelphia, Pennsylvania.

Gathered to Hear the Living Voice

by Gail McGrew Eifrig

Some years ago I woke up, startled into panic because a strange voice was speaking in the bedroom. But it was no masked intruder or other dramatic terror, just the new announcer at the radio station I habitually use for a wake-up alarm. It took several minutes for my heart to stop pounding and several weeks before I felt that voice to be acceptably familiar.

Few of us would doubt the proposition that we are immediately and powerfully affected by voices, and yet this demonstration of its truth did surprise me. I recall being somewhat baffled by the strength of the emotion generated in me by the unfamiliarity of that disembodied voice. But I should not have been surprised; most of us are affected by voices to a far greater degree than we realize. Western culture and its heavy reliance on print media perhaps has masked this quality of our humanity, as we tend to think that the print on the page is simply the equivalent of that spoken word. But our responsiveness to the spoken word is fundamentally and powerfully human. We can

81

be sure that the phone company that urges us to "reach out and touch someone" has based that slogan on the careful study of the extent to which our voices do affect others. Indeed, the very use of the word "touch" in that campaign is a signal of the profound closeness and emotional content inherent in our response to voices.

I suspect that this understanding about the emotional importance of vocal communication underlies our concepts of preaching. Something primitive and elemental focuses in the tradition of preaching—the tribe gathers around the sacred space and listens to the voice that repeats something important, something well-known and yet endlessly repeatable. The voice draws us inward into the group with which we listen, its very familiarity weaving around us a kind of spell, so that we sometimes can fade in and out of the specific content of what is being said at the moment, yet not lose anything of the event. We know how this story comes out because it is our story as much as it is the teller's story. I can recall seeing any number of television programs in which this kind of experience is demonstrated. Despite all the variations and the different configurations of groups—their clothing, hairstyles, pottery, family size, posture, instruments—we can recognize what is happening. In these events, people have gathered to be present at the reiteration of their story, the truths older than any person attending, the collection of truths that makes them who they are. Hearing the truth together, the people take hold of it, they become the identity they profess. If you ever have been a guest at such an event, at a Hopi dance, for instance, you may as an outsider find the quality of repetition almost unbearably tedious. But the fact that the story belongs to a group makes the repetition for them powerfully effective. This is because when we hear *our* story, we never can be bored.

I know that this image drawn from cultures that we consider to be "other" does not accord very well with the theology of preaching taught to the Lutheran pastors I have heard over the years. Good sons of the Reformation most of them (and a few daughters), they've been taught a great deal about the formulations of doctrine. They've been taught about the Bible—its languages, its structures and organization, the history of its exposition and interpretation. They've been taught about the application of biblical truth and confessional understanding to modern life. They've learned a great deal about psychology and the various stresses that can be addressed by confessional formulations, properly understood. The training for preaching, it seems to me, has convinced them that they are supposed to convey all this to me in some winsome and compelling way. I have listened to them struggle to do this for more Sundays than I can count (2,912 says the calculator, and that will do), and I give them much credit for their effort.

But such a concept of preaching seems too much influenced by a part of the Reformation heritage that we might now consider ourselves ready to abandon. We have, as Lutherans, a tradition of preaching that derives most of its goals from the tradition of the academic lecture. It is based on the assumption that the preacher knows more than those being preached to, and should deliver this knowledge in whatever units of time—an hour, or twenty minutes, or ten minutes—the situation allows. While this assumption used to be true, it is no longer the case. For one thing, it simply is a fact that I am better educated than a lot of preachers—not on the basis of my doctorate in literature, but often even in matters of the Bible, Christian history, and the confessions. How often haven't I sat in the pew listening to wrong information, shoddy biblical reading, half-baked pop psychology, incorrect assertions about church history or practice, all of this interspersed with jokes, canned interpretations that are meant to apply to communities wholly unlike the congregation in which I sit, and here and there the odd tag of ghastly pious doggerel. Or, because the more recently educated seminarian has been taught to include his own experience in the sermon, we are subjected to a self-indulgent narrative of

personal trial or insight, often embarrassingly banal, however
heartfelt. Yet, patiently we sit there, silent and resigned, waiting
till the formula that marks the end of the sermon is pro-
nounced, for then we have the promise of returning to that part
of the service that will provide us with what we are there for—
prayer, offering, sacrament, and benediction.

Now some traditions have met this problem by training
preachers toward a different goal. They appear to have said
something such as this: "Since the hearers are probably as educated as the preachers, there is no point in having sermons that
are instructional. What preaching should do is inspire and
excite people about the faith and the way faith could operate in
their lives, if only they were more excited." So now there is, in
some quarters at least, the effort to train preachers to be more
effectively entertaining and inspiring. Some of these people are
good at it, if you like that sort of thing. But if it is painful to
hear a lecture by a not-very-effective lecturer, it is infinitely
worse to be present as a mediocre entertainer attempts to enter-
tain. Better a dreary lecture than a lousy stand-up act.

In view of the potential for disaster, and the numerous
instances of actual failure in what is hoped for from preaching,
why does it continue to be such a central part of the experience
of being a Christian? Here I return to the earlier part of this
essay, to the power of the voice of another person to reach into
the central part of our existence as humans. Though
Christianity has developed a compelling group of rational
descriptions and explanations of the story of salvation through
the loving activity of Jesus Christ in cross and resurrection,
those descriptions find their most compelling form when they
reach us not simply in the written word, but through the voice
of another person. If we were some other kind of being, some
wholly rational creature whose operations were motivated
largely by appeal to the purely intellectual part of our nature,
then perhaps we'd have abandoned the spoken, preached ver-
sion of the gospel long ago. We could read an account, digest

the argument, make our assent, and that would be it. We could
know and believe the gospel without these awkward attempts to
convey it by the human agency of speech. But, framed as we
are, we retain a sense that the word about the Word will work
most potently through the words of a voice. And our sense of
this is so strong that even those people without clear auditory
perception desire to have words conveyed to them through
human agency, even if "voice" is in this case substituted with
those beautiful swift motions of the hands in signed speech.

If I examine my own experience with listening to preaching
and try to give an account of it that is accurate and fair, I want
that account to include both gratitude and hope, along with its
quite evident criticism. I am grateful for preaching that shows
the result of effort and practice. Respecting craft, I believe that
preaching demands the development of skill. The skills of study
belong to preaching (though the admonition not to preach
your preparation is a wise one, I think), and the preacher who
carefully has studied the text will earn my thanks. I am grateful
to preachers who consider who we are, here in the pews, and
who do not rely on the easy sermon-material stuff that comes
from sources ready to sell help to tired clergy. My particular
peeves are the "God is so wonderfully present in the beauty of
nature" sermon preached to the inner-city parish, or the "God
wants all families to be headed by fathers who model themselves on his loving care" sermon preached at the rows of single
mothers, broken families, abandoned husbands, and abused
daughters sitting right there in front of the pulpit. If the generic
is all that is available to the preacher, then I am grateful most of
all for brevity.

These instances of inappropriate sermons are so frequent
that one must, I think, be forced to examine why they occur.
How can it be that a pastor who knows the flock sitting out in
the pews feels a need to rely on those "birdcalls"—the clichéd,
overgeneralized, trite, or canned material that simply sits there
in boilerplate waiting to be assembled into a limp and tedious

sermon? The rationale I would expect (after we had finished
with "I am too busy to prepare a good sermon") from anyone
brave enough to face up to this accusation would be something
like "I'm afraid I'm just not much of a preacher."

I must confess to being persistently puzzled at the development of the church that has led us to expect that the variety of
tasks that should be done among the gathered people of God
are all to be done by the pastor. Since Scripture warrants our
acknowledging a variety of gifts, which can be exercised by a
variety of people for the building up and benefiting of the
whole, why have we organized ourselves doggedly around the
practice that one designated person does all the tasks of ministry? I find it odd that, although a pastor may be very bad at
preaching, we all expect her to stick at *that* task through hell
and high water, as though her ordination conferred on her a
gift that she does not have. Churches need preaching, and they
also need wiring, plumbing, worship leading, carpet cleaning,
flower arranging, bell ringing, tax preparation, Sunday school
teaching, organ playing, visiting of the sick, and pest control.
We know pretty well, after we have been in a congregation for
awhile, whose gifts lie where. Granting every bit of the central-
ity of the proclamation of the Word, why do we believe that
only one person can do it? It seems time to explore ways in
which the pastor, who is certainly responsible for the proclamation of the Word, fulfills that responsibility by finding the
preachers in the congregation and enabling their preaching.
Among other things, the task of listening out for those who
can preach and then working with them on texts, discussing
the craft together, could be a marvelous new area of mutual
growth and enrichment!

I settle down for the sermon, Sunday after Sunday, in hope.
For I *have* heard the good news from the pulpit. The voice of
another human being has reached out, has come into my con-
sciousness through my willingness to listen, and I have been
blessed with hearing the truth of God's love for me. Indeed, I

remember the very sermon in which, for the first time, I heard that and felt it to be true. Certainly I had heard before that God loved me, and I certainly would have assented to that as a proposition, and I certainly believed it to be true. But hearing that sermon I felt it as not only true, but actual. I felt loved by God. I was more than forty, which means that, by that time, my count must have been about two thousand. This experience seems to me evidence for the belief that, for the preacher, there always should be the hope that even what has been heard before, and ignored before, may finally achieve the goal.

Perhaps it someday might be true that we who are gathered into the church might come to see ourselves like those groups of people who gather to hear their story repeated for them by the tellers of the story. They do not come to hear a lecture since they have little to learn in this setting. They do not come to be entertained, to laugh, or to be amazed at skill in speaking, though such qualities would be welcome. They do not come in obedience to the power of the teller. They come because to hear the story is to be revived and fed in the center of their souls. They come because to be there, in the presence of those words, one can know what it is to be one's truest self in being a part of this story. When the preaching of the Christian gospel is what it ought to be, then we hear, in the living voice of a teller, the story of our connection to God through the life and death and rising of Jesus the Christ. That is a simple thing, and it is everything.

➤ ➤ ➤

Gail McGrew Eifrig is a professor of English at Valparaiso University, Valparaiso, Indiana, and is a lecturer on the topic of preaching.

TELLING

Speaking Is Our Holy Task

by April Ulring Larson

f I say, 'I will not mention him, or speak any more in his name,' there is in my heart as it were a burning fire shut up in my bones, and I am weary with holding it in, and I cannot" (Jeremiah 20:9, RSV).

What do we do with this word of God that makes our heart pound? We cannot help it. We must speak of Jesus or burst. "We cannot keep from speaking about what we have seen and heard" (Acts 4:20). "'[Jesus] even makes the deaf hear and the dumb speak'" (Mark 7:37, RSV). God's call is clear. This sending out of all of us to proclaim the good news is one common theme occurring in all four Gospels. The church is a people called and sent.

Jesus sends us many times. In Matthew, he uses these words: "'Go . . . make disciples . . . baptizing . . . and teaching'" (28:19-20) and "As you go, proclaim the good news, 'The kingdom of heaven has come near.' Cure the sick, raise the dead, cleanse the lepers, cast out demons" (10:7). Other examples are found in Mark: "Go, tell"(16:7); in Luke: "Repentance and forgiveness of sins is to be proclaimed in his name to all nations, beginning from Jerusalem"(24:47); in Acts: "You will receive power when the Holy Spirit has come upon you; and you will be my witnesses in Jerusalem, in all Judea and Samaria, and to the ends of the earth" (1:8); and finally in John: "'Peace be with you. As the Father has sent me, so send I you'" (20:21). Christians have heard in Moses' frustrated words a longing for the day when all of God's people would be called as proclaimers: "'Would that all the LORD's people were prophets, and that the LORD would put his spirit on them!'" (Numbers 11:29). To speak the word is our *holy task.* To proclaim the Word of Jesus Christ is an awesome responsibility to which every single Christian is called and sent. Sisters and brothers, thank you for proclaiming the Word. I need to hear it from you.

After my election as a synodical bishop, I requested that pastors and lay people lead devotions and prayer before every committee meeting. A highlight of my synodical work is to hear my brothers and sisters in Christ proclaim the good news of Jesus Christ to me and to all those gathered around the conference table.

Preaching begins in listening, which is a difficult task. This listening includes listening to God, listening to the body of Christ, and listening to the cries of the world.

Preparation to preach begins in studying and listening to the text, not dissecting it. We do not stand over the text; the text stands over us. The Bible pierces our lives and the lives of the world as we carefully study and listen to the text. We are not scientists dissecting the text. The text stands over us embracing and challenging all of us who bear Christ's mark upon our brow. It is not that we capture the Word, but that the Word captures us.

So I come with you, my brothers and sisters, kneeling beside you in the pew, bringing my joys, my brokenness, my disappointments, my shame, my guilt, to our triune God witnessed in the Scriptures and coming and dwelling with us as Jesus

Christ. I sit with you, unprotected, often feeling exposed and
without defense as we encounter the living God. This God is
passionately, extravagantly, recklessly in love with you and with
me and with the world. In the midst of a society that demands,
"Be all that you can be," God announces, "You are mine. Be all
that you are."

How does one speak of such a God, who seems to think it is
okay to love anyone? I stand and sit with you in bursting thank-
fulness that our God loves us, extravagantly and without condi-
tions. In God's extravagant love I take my place with all the
baptized as one who receives the Word along with the bread
and wine as grace and pure gift from God.

In addition to this most important gift of being a child of
God, God and the church has called me to be a pastor and a
bishop. How is it that I take my place first as one of the baptized
to receive the Word, but also by God's grace called to proclaim
and to feed those who feed, care, and proclaim to the world? I
look out at these people in every congregation in which I have
been asked to preach and am amazed that I have the joy, task,
and privilege of proclaiming to all God's people our great gift
in Jesus Christ.

The problem with preaching is that God keeps getting in the
way. God is messy. God changes God's mind. The reason
preaching is so difficult is you keep running into God. *God* is
the problem. It's not that speaking is so difficult. It is not that
filling up twenty minutes with words is so difficult. God is the
problem. God gets in the way and makes an interesting, challenging task an impossible one.

The difficulty of the task is a lot like childbearing. Like
childbirth, preaching is a mystery. Even though I have
preached thousands of sermons and delivered only three
babies, I believe I know even less about preaching than childbirth. The birth of babies is like the birth of a sermon in
which people experience new life. Both are mysteries. God
does God's thing. We can't control it. It is a gift to be a parent.

It is a gift to be a pastor and preach to the baptized, to
encourage the encouragers, to feed those who feed the world
with the good news and the bread of life.

Over and over again as I study and prepare to preach, I come
back to the question: What would you have me say, God? There
is just this little bit of time. What should I say? How does this
text connect to their lives? God has a word for the people. There
is a connection. I need to listen. Study and listen. Pause and listen. Read the text again and listen. Have someone else read the
text out loud to me and listen. In the same way, think of the
people, the community, our suffering world, specific individuals, and families, and listen. Finally, I listen to myself encountered by the text. The Bible is so disturbing. What are you saying here? Where are you taking us, God? What is the Spirit
doing? Can I articulate even a bit of that?

If the Spirit of God could be boxed, if the Spirit of God
would allow herself to be rationed out evenly to everyone in fair
portions, "but the Spirit blows where the Spirit wills." *God is the
problem.* God gets in the way. You are working on the text and
you're doing all the things that you've been taught to do. You
pray, translate the text, read it in context (going back and reading several chapters before and after, maybe the whole book),
you ask questions of the text and check words in the Greek lexi-
con and concordance, you reflect and reflect and reflect, asking
yourself, "What are the issues here?" After doing many hours of
faithful study, you may then turn to those revered scholars and
teachers in the church, reading their commentaries on these
texts. You may find comfort in the words of an eminent biblical
scholar. For a moment or maybe a few hours, you have an
answer, an angle. You have solved the issue. You have a solution,
and everything fits neatly into a pattern, but God gets in the
way. One of the ways God gets in the way is through the holy
community, the communion of saints, the community of the
baptized. Sometimes the children are the worst. They ask out
loud questions that good Christian adults have since learned

not to ask: Where does evil come from? Why do people suffer? Why are some people wealthy and others poor? If God is good, why is there so much suffering? Why does God allow and encourage so much killing in the Old Testament? These core impossible questions go on and on. The holy community is the problem, or it's at least our children who enunciate out loud the unanswered questions in our hearts and minds. It is true, creation is broken. We confess on Sunday, "We are in bondage to sin and cannot free ourselves."

This is the world you and I see—the weak die, the strong survive. The wealthy get wealthier, the poor get poorer. Violence in families increases as poverty increases. The first are first and the last are last.

The suffering may be caused by us, but what makes preaching difficult is not standing up in front of people speaking about God. The problem is God, or at least it is the God as revealed in Scripture. What do you do with a Bible that tells us God never changes, and then tells us God changes God's mind? Our God is a God who cannot be tamed, a God who stirs the waters and quiets the waters, a God who creates and destroys, a God who drowns and raises, a God who can be called on by name and a God who does not come at my demand. This is a God who creates chaos and order. Our God is an unsafe God and a God who is revealed in Scripture in sometimes opposite ways and words. This untamed God says to the Christian, "Proclaim me and proclaim my deeds." This God who holds us, keeps us, embraces us, protects us, and always pays attention to us is still an unsafe God. Perhaps our biggest temptation when we preach and when any of us baptized Christians speak of God is to make this unsafe God safe, this tameless God tame. We walk in a world where the first is first and the last is last, but the preacher is called by the gospel to preach instead this incomprehensible word, "Some are last who will be first, and some are first who will be last" (Luke 13:30). And it is not just a far-off word for that final day when Christ returns. Jesus already has ushered in a new day. The kingdom has come in Jesus. Wherever the last are first and the first are last, wherever the blind see and those who have never listened before listen, these are moments of God's kingdom come among us.

And so, my dear sisters and brothers, let us pray for the preacher. As people of faith, God's own people, we gather again this week. The pastor's charge is clear. Point us again to Jesus. Every Sunday, over and over, tell us the same story of Jesus and his love. Remind us with many verbs how deeply we are loved by God. Pastor, preach Christ that we may believe. Pastor, lead us in our daily calls to proclaim and live your word. Call us to the table. Call us to our hungry neighbor. Call us to proclaim Christ in deed and word.

➤ ➤ ➤

April Ulring Larson, a noted preacher, serves as bishop of the LaCrosse Area Synod of the Evangelical Lutheran Church in America.

God's Love Story Is Dialogue

by Walter Wangerin Jr.

One Sunday the bishop came to town. He came to accomplish a number of tasks, but chiefest among them (as far as *we* were concerned) was to preach at the morning worship service at Grace Lutheran Church.

His chiefest experience of the day, I verily believe, occurred during that same worship service, in which he preached a sermon through which he learned something about preaching.

From 1974 to the later '80s, Grace was my parish, my community—and my teacher. It's a small inner-city church whose membership in those days was mostly African American. They *live* in the verbal exchange. Talk is life. And dialogue for them is the most complex, the truest means of human engagement. I studied homiletics in the seminary, but it was Grace that taught me how to preach.

Fundamental to their sense of the sermon is that it is not, nor can it be, merely a monologue—one person speaking, one person controlling the whole of this communication. Nor, if the sermon *is* conceived of as dialogue, can it be a dialogue between the preacher and the manuscript—the written word and the spoken word interfacing, as it were. (But this is precisely the sort of "dialogue" that occurs when preachers pay more attention to the notes below their faces than to the people gazing back at them.)

"Amen! Amen!" So they spoke their word to the better word that I had uttered. And they laughed aloud. And they frowned and pinched their lips and raised their hands and, and, most demanding of all. . . .

Bishop Harold Hecht was a fireplug of a man, short, bright, erect, his energy awaiting but the twist of a reason to shoot forth streams of language. That's the way he preached—rising to his toes, rising to rhetorical heights. And that's how he preached at Grace the Sunday he came to our town. He took to the pulpit as to horses and a Roman chariot. He also (so we saw for the first time) felt bound to a particular, preestablished pattern—notes. The sermon the bishop was preaching was fixed. It was finished before it began.

So as he rounded the first corner—sermonic point number one—with an illustration and a rhetorical question, three parishioners opened their mouths and then closed them, their eyes baffled under the thunder of this galloping messenger. So then he charged around the second point, again with the story, again with the question, and seven members opened their mouths.

But when the bishop hit the third point with a third rhetorical question, Mike Magan, twelve years old, could tolerate the monologue no longer. He jumped to his feet and *answered* the question and knocked poor Harold off his horses, down to the ground where the pews and the people were. *Fap, fap, fapple, fap.* As if riding a flat tire, the bishop slowed and stopped and focused on the kid who was standing before him.

Perforce, the preacher now took into account a speaking people. Harold, dear man, had the grace to laugh at himself;

and then, with less polish and greater fumbling, but with greater attention to the folks before him, he spoke his holy word within the community rather than at it.

➤ ➤ ➤

Now I host *Lutheran Vespers*. I am deeply grateful for this ministry. It is of God.

But if I had not spent decades in pastoral intimacy with a congregation, preaching "Sun-daily" before the same faces, preaching to those whose lives I shared the week long, I doubt that I now could understand how to preach over the radio to people I do not see.

It seems to me that there are but two fundamental requirements of the parish preacher, without which the purpose and the goodness and the godliness of preaching are distorted and disappointed.

The first goes to the preacher's heart and passions—that the subject of her sermon be more important to her than anything else in her life, anything else in this world.

- The more she's convinced of her subject's importance, the more will she be compelled to draw on her best resources to communicate it—all her intellect, all her verbal skills, all the personal force of her character. And then she will not mimic the preaching of others; rather, she will find her own best voice, gesture, language.
- The more her subject is crucial to her own being, her own life and faith, the more will she be completely present in the preaching. No acting, then. No rote, no fulfilling of ritual alone, no hum-drummy repetition of a job's assignment; rather, this preacher will be authentic in the dialogue. She herself will be there and available to all who hear her.

Moreover, if her subject is the very staff of her life, she will not be shoddy in her thought regarding it. She will with every fiber in her being desire to "get it right." She will search and research its truth, its complexity, never to offer the thing of her greatest passions cheaply. She will prepare sermons with her whole mind and the best of her reading and education.

The first principle of real preaching, in other words—in better words—is this: You shall love the Lord your God with all your heart, and with all your soul, and with all your mind. And choose no other subject for your preaching *except* this Lord and God.

My father-in-law was all his life a farmer. By his ninth decade—a father of fourteen children, a grandfather and great-grandfather of a small congregation—much of his life force had abated. He had never studied communications. His formal education had ceased at the eighth grade. He was by his very nature retiring and quiet.

Nevertheless, when Martin Bohlmann wanted to utter something of holy significance, he could command the rapt attention of his entire family. He would lean forward and lower his voice to the tones of a common man filled with awe—a tone peculiar to Martin alone. You see? The subject, beloved by Martin, heart, soul, and mind, made of Martin a preacher of moving authenticity.

Love Jesus. And preach Jesus. This is the greatest and the first requirement.

And the second is like unto it.

This goes to the preacher's eyes, his attentions, and his deepest purposes—that the righteousness, the consolations, the health, and the salvation of those unto whom he preaches are as vital to him as his own.

The first requirement refers to the *what* of preaching. The second refers to the *why.*

The first makes real the news to the preacher. The second makes real the hearers to the preacher, in order that he may make real the news to these particular hearers, too.

And this is what I learned at Grace Church: You shall love your neighbor as yourself. I should love *these* members, these particular Christians, this present congregation as much as I love my own health and salvation.

They simply would not allow me to avoid or else ignore
their dense human detail. And because of the genuine, clam-
orous urgency of their listening, my preaching was perforce to
them.

And because I preached to them of the thing I loved above
all other things, I loved those so involved in receiving it.

And because I loved *them,* I did not preach to the air, as it
were, sending out my words like rain to fall anywhere upon the
place beneath. Nor did I preach to some idealized (but unreal)
audience; no, I could not even prepare my sermons for people
in general, for some imagined congregation, as if sermons
could be interchangeable from place to place. (Let's see, I have a
slam-dunk Easter sermon on this text, and this church hasn't
heard it before. Time to preach it again.)

Rather, when I preached, I had to look at the people in
front of me, because they were the reason of my preaching. I
found I moved from the pulpit in order to be literally nearer
them since I wanted them to receive this most important thing
I had to say. I adjusted delivery to their faces, their words,
their postures, their listening. Of course, they demanded that
it be dialogue!

But in order to preach such a sermon, I first had to study the
texts with this people in mind. I had to prepare the sermon for
the members of Grace as they were in that particular week.

And to *know* them that week, I had to be among them, pay-
ing a constant, watchful attention, speaking with them, listening to them.

And in order to know them that week, I had to know them
in the fullness of their lives—how they furnished their houses,
where they worked, what they thought, how they experienced
pleasure and pain, what sins they sinned, what sorrows they
endured, what joys had come to lift them up.

Love God. And love *this* people, the persons of this parish.
On these two fundamental principles hangs the whole of holy
preaching.

➤ ➤ ➤

When I began preaching for *Lutheran Vespers,* John Peterson, director for public media of the Evangelical Lutheran Church in America, asked me a curious question, "What space will you inhabit?"

What space? Why, a radio booth, isn't that obvious? I'll sit several inches back from a microphone, hunched above my Bible on a table.

Well, no, that isn't what John had in mind.

"In what context will people receive your words?" he asked. "Where is the *place* of your speaking?"

Suddenly I understood his question and my answer. Moreover, I understood how radio could accomplish the two great commandments of preaching.

I had feared that a radio ministry might undermine my love for particular persons. After all, I can't see those to whom I preach. You are ears alone, and I am a voice alone; it is but the air between us.

But I chose not to answer John's question in this way: "I inhabit an imaginary pulpit, and my listeners imaginary pews. We are in church." Most religious radio programs present sermons as if they were uttered in a formal place. They run the danger, then, of preaching *at* people—the monologue.

Instead I have chosen to be where you are.

What is the context of our encounter, the speaking and the listening? Why, wherever your radio is. In the kitchen, in the car, in the bedroom early in the morning or late at night, in the barn while you do the chores. I am with you, and you bring to our dialogue the details. I speak to you as if I were in the same room, a few feet away. I speak as if there were no more than two or three listening. I will not shout at you. I will not raise my voice to "more than a million listeners" since none of you is the million-headed monster. And all this I do because it allows Jesus' love to become love between us two.

I learned the truer numbers at Grace.

And Grace Lutheran Church, by inviting me for so many years into the true interior of the members' lives, by being honest and unashamed, and by loving me in return, has taught me, too, the details of *your* lives, dear listeners. To have known one people exceedingly well is to have discovered the individual lives of many peoples.

Now *Lutheran Vespers* is celebrating fifty years of radio ministry. Oh, how grateful I am to the Lord God for preserving the Word in the air this way.

And how grateful I am to the holy people of God who have welcomed poor preachers into their hearts and souls and minds, for it is ever in dialogue that the Word is heard among us, ever in dialogue that preaching is made real.

➤ ➤ ➤

Walt Wangerin, master storyteller and prize-winning author, is the current speaker on Lutheran Vespers.